# THE
# PRIESTHOOD
# OF MAN

Anthony D. Duncan

3.8.74

Joy and Peace.

Geoffrey Bles

*The Priesthood of Man*
is published by
Geoffrey Bles
59 Brompton Road, London SW3 IDS

ISBN: 0 7138 0670 2

© Anthony D. Duncan, 1973

Printed by Butler & Tanner Ltd
Frome and London

# Preface

If I were a scholar, I should have found it more difficult to write this book than I did, for it seeks to explore a number of those corners into which the academic hesitates to venture—and not without reason.

My concern is with what we call "Heaven" and what we call "Earth" and the place of man in relation to both. Being a Christian, and having in some senses "seen Christ", I am bound to see everything else in His light, and perfected in Him. I make no bones about this for it stems from conversion, conviction and experience.

I am indebted to many friends and teachers. I readily acknowledge the source of the best of chapters 14, 15 and 16 to be three unpublished lectures given by Professor D. E. Nineham at Chichester Theological College in Holy Week, 1961. The imagery in chapter 21 is borrowed with thanks from the Reverend Canon Andrew Glazewski, and without the timely discovery of Claud Chavasse's little book, *The Bride of Christ*, to back up and in some cases correct my own thoughts, chapters 17 and 18 would have been much the poorer.

I have borrowed almost the whole of a chapter from an earlier book of my own, *The Whole Christ* (S.P.C.K. 1968) to provide the framework of chapters 19, 20 and 22.

Chapters 13, 23 and 24 will cause some eyebrows to rise, but I am committed to what I have written.

I am particularly indebted to my friends Dorothy M. Arnold and Gareth Knight for their labours in reading and criticising the original manuscript, and to Brigid Rowsell for compiling the index. And to many others for their prayers and encouragement.

A. D. D.

Highnam Rectory, Gloucester.

## NOTE

The Biblical references are all from the Jerusalem Bible unless noted otherwise.

The references from the Koran are from the Penguin edition, translated by N. J. Dawood.

The versions of the Vedas, the Upanishads and the Gita are those of the Penguin edition, translated by Juan Mascaro.

The renderings of the Tau Teh Ching are my own (after Lin Yutang).

# Contents

*Part One*

Concerning the Earth

# I

# Heaven and Earth

In his letter to the Christian community at Philippi, St Paul quoted a hymn to Jesus Christ. He may or may not have been the author of it, but it contains the words:

> ". . . God raised him high
> and gave him the name
> which is above all other names
> so that all beings
> in the heavens, on earth and in the underworld,
> should bend the knee at the name of Jesus . . ."
>
> (*Phil. 2:9, 10*)

The words "in the heavens, on earth and in the underworld", are reminiscent of the generally accepted opinion that the ancients thought in terms of a "three-tier universe". We have inherited, from the preceding centuries, many presuppositions based upon later Christian (or supposedly Christian) understandings, and we are not aware of the extent to which we project back into the past what we ourselves take for granted, nor do we take sufficient account of the extent to which our approaches are preconditioned by the climate of opinion in which we have been brought up. We take for granted the Christian orthodoxy of our presuppositions whereas we should do very well to question even this more often than we do. And so, in a work which will seek to explore what I shall describe, for want of better terms, as the relationship between what we call "heaven" and what we call "earth", I shall begin at what must be the beginning for Christians and Jews: the Creation Myth of the first chapter of Genesis.

"In the beginning God created the heavens and the earth."

These words, the very first in the Holy Bible, will serve admirably to begin this work, for not only do they set the metaphysical stage for the rest of Holy Scripture, they will be found to be a very sure foundation, and a touchstone, for much that will follow. Definition of terms will emerge during the course of the book, for it must be remembered that the priestly editors of the Pentateuch, assembling the Hebrew sacred writings into a coherent whole in the enforced leisure of their exile, made no attempt whatever to define the terms they used. The reason for this is quite simple; their minds did not work that way. As R. H. Lightfoot perceived, "the Jews valued, above all, will and action in the expression of life, the Greeks assigned the highest place to intellect and thought."[1] It does not matter very much, therefore, what the editors of Genesis imagined "the heavens" and "the earth" to be—if indeed they exercised their imaginations in this matter —because the one thing that mattered to them was the revealed purpose of God being worked out in the context of such orders of creation as they perceived.

Scholars derive both pleasure and profit from arguing among themselves as to whether the Genesis Creation Myths (there are two) indicate belief in creation *ex nihilo*, or of creation from pre-existent matter. It might thus be argued that both myths (Chapters One and Two of Genesis) suggest that God created an ordered cosmos out of pre-existent chaos, but it would be unrealistic to construct too much of an argument upon this for the simple reason that the Hebrew editors borrowed both myths from their Semitic neighbours. Of the two myths, the second is the older, but the first is the more important by far, for it is a very important recasting of the framework of the Babylonian Epic of Creation. The metaphysical framework was used to provide the background against which the editors could express their own distinctive and dynamic understanding of the purposes of God as revealed in the process of creation.

It matters hardly at all when or from whom this myth came into Hebrew hands; very probably it was familiar to them long before the Exile, perhaps from their Canaanite neighbours. What matters supremely is what they did with it when they had got it. Unique to the

[1] R. H. Lightfoot, *St John's Gospel: A Commentary*, O.U.P., p. 53.

Hebrew understanding was a sense of history; the sense of a purpose unfolding itself in the march of events. All through the Old Testament the hope is for a glorious and fulfilling future which will contrast splendidly with the often frustrating and tormented present. The eschatological hope of Israel was quite earthbound, and very materialistic in concept. God would intervene gloriously in the affairs of men, but his intervention would remain earthly, because earth is the abode of men. The best hope of Israel, classically, was for divinely ordered "good times" in the future. The sheer, steadfast materialism of the Children of Israel is, all too often, quite lost sight of.

A process was at work in creation; the rest of mankind could have their myths which expressed, often with great beauty and profundity, a once-for-all, static concept of creation; they might rest secure in their "as it-was-in-the-beginning-is-now-and-ever-shall-be" philosophies, but Israel knew things to be different. A process was observable, God's will was dynamic; he acted, and his will for man in general and Hebrew man in particular was being unfolded and made manifest in the course of history. The priest-editors of the Exile might be described, with some justice, as the first of the "process theologians"; but the entire Old Testament is "process theology" from end to end!

The editors of Genesis state that "God created the heavens and the earth"; what was their understanding of these terms, "the heavens" and "the earth"? Does our understanding differ sufficiently markedly for such difference to matter? "The heavens" (or heaven) has, throughout the Old Testament, much the same variety of meanings as it has for us today. Thus "the heavens" might mean the sky (in English, this usage is usually confined to poetry), but at the same time it denotes the abode, or place, or state of God and his angels.

In poetry and in popular piety the two meanings are run together, and God is referred to as being, in some sense, "up there". It was in alarm lest this confusion of meanings be taken literally in the present age that Bishop John Robinson wrote his well-known book *Honest to God*. But in fact it is probable that few people today take such poetic licence as literal truth. "The heavens and the earth", therefore, mean two distinct pairs of concepts. The first is "the created universe in general and the planet earth in particular", and the second is "the unimaginable *milieu* of God on the one hand and creation as we understand that word upon the other". It is certain that in the pre-scientific and very unmetaphysical minds of the priest-editors of Genesis, the two sets of meanings were held in the merriest confusion; it is equally certain that this high probability is of no consequence to us whatsoever.

The ancients undoubtedly believed in a "three-tier universe", but they did not hold this view in quite the way in which we tend to imagine they did.

The abode of God and of his angels—the "Sons of God" of *Job 1:6, 2:1*—was indeed believed to be located somewhere beyond the visible sky, and a doctrine of various stages of "the heavens" emerged (varying somewhat from one school of thought to another), to which St Paul refers in his description, to the Christians at Corinth, of the graces given to him in prayer: "I know a man in Christ who, fourteen years ago, was caught up—whether still in the body or out of the body, I do not know; God knows—right into the third heaven." (*2 Cor 12:1, 2.*) But there is an inherent difficulty in trying to say anything about heaven. Dictionaries refer, unsatisfactorily, to a "state or place", and neither term will satisfy. Man can only describe the indescribable in terms of symbols which are meaningful to him and arise from his own, earthly, condition. Thus the subjective response and counterpart to objective mystical experience must be expressed in terms which are part of the common currency of mankind. A wholly transcending, wholly "other" objective awareness will provoke a subjective expression which is visual or pictorial to some minds and audible to others, but in either event the response must be anthropomorphic in character. In Jacob's dream, "a ladder was there, standing on the ground with its top reaching to heaven" (*Gen 28:12*); and in the collective experience of the Disciples at our Lord's Ascension, "he was lifted up while they looked on, and a cloud took him from their sight" (*Acts 1:9*). The objective experience and the certain understanding that comes from it are one thing; the subjective expression or "clothing" of it is quite another. The two must be recognised as complementary but quite separate.

In the Old Testament there is almost no suggestion that man should ever "go to heaven". Heaven was not seen as being in any sense the abode of mankind and there are only two exceptions to this rule in the whole canon of the Old Testament. The first is the shadowy, patriarchal figure of Enoch who, long before the Flood, "walked with God. Then he vanished because God took him." (*Gen 5:24.*) The second exception is the colourful and far more familiar figure of Elijah, who, at the end of his prophetic ministry, went out into the desert with his chosen successor, Elisha. "A chariot of fire appeared and horses of fire, coming between the two of them; and Elijah went up to heaven in the whirlwind." (*2 Kings 2:11.*) In the first century of the Christian era, "The Assumption of Moses" was written, but it was a tract for the times rather than an assertion of doctrine. Throughout the Old Testament, the idea of heaven was quite "other" and was not a state or place to which men could expect to aspire.

Having said this, however, it must be remembered that Jewish tradition maintains that two *Torahs* ("instructions" as opposed to "laws") were given on Sinai. The Pentateuch represents the written Torah—the formal skeleton of Judaism—and the second was the oral Torah which is the living, developing, organic body; the living commentary and interpretation of the written Torah which keeps it alive and relevant to Jews in all ages. Within the Oral Torah, as it developed over the centuries, there accumulated a wealth of mystical and occult tradition of which a non-Jew would have very little conception. It is somewhat hazardous, therefore, to make absolute statements as to the belief of a whole people over a thousand years of their history before Christ. Suffice it to say that the text of the Old Testament supports the conclusion that heaven was not typically conceived of as the desired end of man.

I have referred to a "three-tier universe", but Genesis tells of the emergence of two "orders" of creation only; "the heavens" and "the earth". What, then, of that third place or state to which, in the translation of the Authorised Version, is given the dread name of hell?

It must be confessed that the Authorised Version is, in this respect, most seriously misleading. Added to this, the influence of Calvinism over the last four centuries has contributed to a notion of hell which is a grave, and unbiblical misconception, at least in so far as the Old Testament is concerned. The English word "hell" is used to translate two completely different concepts. The first is the place or state of ultimate retribution for ultimate sin. Most of the references to hell in the New Testament carry this meaning and are a rendering of "Gehenna", the "Valley of Hinnom" to the south and south-west of Jerusalem, anciently a place of pagan human sacrifice to Moloch. The mediaeval authority Kimchi says that fires were kept burning constantly for refuse. Our Lord used Gehenna as a name for the state of final punishment, taking it from a late Jewish tradition such as is expressed in 2 Esdras. "Then the place of torment shall appear . . . the furnace of hell shall be displayed." (*NEB 7:36*.) He warns men, lest they should "go to hell, into the fire that cannot be put out" (*Mk 9:43*); or lest they should be told in the end, "Go away from me, with your curse upon you, to the eternal fire prepared for the devil and his angels." (*Matt 25:41*.) Hell, in this punitive sense, is almost entirely a New Testament concept. This is not the understanding behind the word rendered "hell" in the Old Testament, and I shall return to this point in the final section of this book.

The second concept, translated by the same word "hell" in the Authorised Version, is, in Hebrew, "*Sheol*" and in Greek, "*Hades*". Both these words refer to the "underworld" or abode of the dead. This is that "hell" which is meant in all the Old Testament references, and which is specifically referred to in a number of important New Testament references to which we shall turn in due course. There is no suggestion of moral judgement attached to Sheol; it is quite simply a place or a state of affairs.

Scholars argue about the degree of belief in continued life after death according to Old Testament evidence. The references differ:

> "The dead cannot praise Yahweh,
> They have gone down to silence:"
> (*Ps 115:17*)

This seems to indicate a belief that the dead are either no longer conscious in any way, or that they are no longer in a position to worship. Yet God is by no means confined within all or any part of his creation, as is proclaimed by Solomon's cry, "Will God really live with men on the earth? Why the heavens and their own heavens cannot contain you." (*1 Kings 8:27*.) The Psalmist asks,

> "Where could I go to escape your spirit?
> Where could I flee from your presence?
> If I climb the heavens, you are there,
> There too, if I lie in Sheol."
> *(Ps 139:7, 8)*

But the answer to the scholars' questions lies outside the realm of academic scholarship, for primitive society is always psychically orientated to a high degree, and spiritism and mediumistic activity is both widespread and commonplace. There is no doubt about the reality of conscious or semi-conscious survival of bodily death among primitive people; they know from common experience that it is so. Mediumistic activity had no place in Hebrew religion, for reasons which we shall discover later on, and this very fact is of extraordinary significance as it represents an almost unique attitude among pre-Christian religions; but Saul indulged in a widespread, if illicit, activity when he said to his servants, "Find a woman who is a necromancer for me to go and consult her." To the medium herself, he said, "Disclose the future to me . . . by means of a ghost. Conjure up the one I shall name to you." (*1 Sam 28:7, 8*.) The ghost of the prophet Samuel, sought by Saul, abode in Sheol, the place of the dead, not in Gehenna, the place of eternal punishment!

The three-tier universe is now seen to conform better with the statement that, in the beginning, God created the heavens and the earth, for the earth is seen as being provided with a "basement", the "depths of Sheol" (*Ps 86:13, Deut 32:22*). Man, in the Old Testament is essentially earthbound. Earth is his place in the scheme of things, with a life of worship and activity followed by a shadowy existence, as it were on "half pay" in the underworld. Thus when Saul's medium saw "a ghost rising up from the earth . . . an old man coming up . . . wrapped in a cloak", it was to pass on a sharp rebuke to her client:

"Why have you disturbed my rest, conjuring me up?" (*1 Sam 28:13ff.*)

Man is an earthbound creature according to the Old Testament; life on earth and rest in Sheol are his lot. But gradually there emerged a belief that this was not to be all. Martha proclaims, in respect of her dead brother Lazarus, "I know he will rise again at the resurrection on the last day" (*Jn 11:25*); and new insights and hopes began to abound at the end of the Old Testament period.

The word Paradise, which must also be considered, is probably Persian in origin and denotes a pleasure-garden, an enclosed park. In this sense it (or its Greek equivalent) occurs in the Greek-language Septuagint text of the Old Testament to describe the primaeval innocence of the second creation myth, that of Adam and Eve and the Fall, in chapters two and three of Genesis. Paradise, in this sense, denotes primaeval innocence. But in later usage, outside the canon of Scripture, it denotes a state of future blessedness which was material and worldly in the Rabbinic texts, and spiritual in the Psalms of Solomon and in parts of Ecclesiasticus.[1] In the New Testament it occurs three times; St Paul's use of the word (*2 Cor 12:4*) and the reference in Revelations (*Rev 2:7*) make Paradise synonymous with the "heaven of the blessed". But the one really well-known use of the word is our Lord's promise to the penitent thief, "today you will be with me in paradise:" (*Lk 23:43*), and it is not absolutely clear what our Lord meant by it, and little advantage may be gained at this stage by speculating upon it. I shall return to this last idea of Paradise later in this work.

The Hebrews, then, were no metaphysicians; they borrowed much of their essential mythology from others, adapting what they borrowed to express their quite distinctive and unique awareness of the dynamic purposes of God in his creation. God and his angels inhabit a state or place called "the heavens", man inhabits "the earth" (with its underworld). The two orders of creation, the milieu of God and the milieu of man are quite separate and "other". But God is not contained

---

[1] *Oxford Dictionary of the Christian Church.*

within all or any part of his creation. He is omnipresent and unimaginable by man:

> "Can you claim to grasp the mystery of God,
> To understand the perfection of Shaddai?
> It is higher than the heavens: what can you do?
> It is deeper than Sheol: what can you know?"
>
> (*Job 11:7, 8*)

There is a dynamic relationship between the heavens and earth; God communicates with man through angelic messengers (variously interpreted throughout the Old Testament), by "visions in the night", by direct inspiration and by mystical experience. Above all, God communicates his will to man through the Law, given on Sinai, the basis of the Covenant relationship between God and the People of God.

But what about the People of God? What, indeed, about the place of man himself in the scheme of things? Earthbound he might be, but he is the supreme creature of the earthly order of creation. In a very real sense he stands between the two worlds, for,

> "God said, 'Let us make man in our own image, in the likeness of ourselves, and let them be masters of the fish of the sea, the birds of heaven, the cattle, all the wild beasts and all the reptiles that crawl upon the earth!" (*Gen 1:26*)

Man is made as one capable of knowing God—about this Genesis could hardly be more clear—of entering into a personal relationship with God, on behalf of that order of created being of which he is the ultimate refinement. To mankind, God says:

"Be fruitful, multiply, fill the earth and conquer it" (*Gen 1:28*) and it is to Adam (mankind) that God brings all the creatures that he has made upon earth for mankind to give them the names which are in themselves the summing-up of their being. Man reigns supreme, under God, over the earth, an image and likeness of God over the lower of the two orders of God's creation. The place of man in Genesis is perfectly clear; he is prophet, priest and King.

Man, in short, is God's manager over the world of which he is a part. But he is more than this, for he is God's priest to the whole of that order of being called "the earth". How then, may priesthood be defined?

A priest is one who stands between two worlds. It is not sufficient that the two worlds meet in him—which, in a sense, they do—nor is it sufficient for him to dwell in one world and look to another. He must stand between the worlds, isolated to a large degree from both, and be at the same time the "door" from one to the other. This is the vision of the place of man in the earliest pages of Genesis, that is the function for which he was called into being. As the Great High Priest of the Gospels said of himself and of his function:

> "I tell you most solemnly,
> I am the gate of the sheepfold."
>
> (Jn 10:7)

And elsewhere,

> "I am the Way, the Truth and the Life.
> No one can come to the Father except through me."
>
> (Jn 14:6)

The place of the priest is at the crossing of Time and Eternity, and he must become identified with the cross of that crossing. It was thus not for nothing that the Curé d'Ars once said, "God made man in the shape of a cross."

# 2

# The Idea of the "Within"

Siddhartha Gautama, the saintly Nepalese prince who is now known to mankind as the Buddha, or "enlightened one", evolved and taught a profound moral philosophy and way of life as the direct result of a mystical experience of great profundity. Born and brought up a Hindu, he later broke with Hinduism because of what he considered to be its obsessive concern for metaphysics. For metaphysics, Buddha cared little; the four Noble Truths and the Eightfold Path were quite sufficient for mortal man to get on with. The thing that matters is the way a man lives, not the profundity of his metaphysical speculation; that this is so few reasoning men will deny, and Buddha proclaimed it emphatically.

Inevitably perhaps, the teachings of the Buddha were turned by lesser men into an *ism*, and as the years passed a Buddhist metaphysic —remarkably like the Hindu—emerged to be taken for granted by good Buddhists as being of the essence of things.

For the Buddha, morals followed upon mystical experience; indeed they were the inevitable consequence of it. The transcending reality disclosed to the mystic's vision made the moral philosophy not merely inevitable, but positively pressing and most vital. In very much the same way the mystical experiences that lie behind the stories in Exodus issued in a strict moral code which was perceived as the essential basis of a personal relationship with a personal God.

Morals have to do with behaviour, and with the motives for behaviour, in relationships between persons. Buddha had no clear revelation about a personal Creator-God, but the Buddhist way of life is consequent upon the perception of a moral order, a kind of "cosmic justice" within the metaphysical concepts the Buddha inherited and which his later followers largely endorsed.

Mystical experience is always prior to a rationally perceived moral order; it is also prior to serious metaphysical speculation, because the task of the metaphysician is to seek to arrive at a reasonable understanding of the underlying framework of things which is consistent (or seems to be consistent) with that which has been mystically perceived in the first instance. It might well be said that the metaphysician is seeking a context—or at least a rationally viable image of a context—for himself and for the world as a whole.

Metaphysics can very easily become an end in itself, and the subject invites rarified academicism of all kinds. Buddha would have none of it. Jesus Christ outlined no metaphysic; indeed there is something faintly absurd about the thought that perhaps he might have done if he had wished. Metaphysics is a necessarily purely human activity; it tends always to debase a vision to the level of an *ism*. But if mystical experience is prior to both morals and metaphysics, then mysticism should be adequately defined. For it is clear that nothing could be more essentially "mystical" in nature than the priesthood, standing as it does between two worlds.

The words mysticism, mystical and mystic mean a large number of different things to different people. They are used in the loosest fashion imaginable. To very many people, they have a vague, romantic and slightly "misty" connotation; to others, the words are occult, and to writers of text-books on ascetic and mystical theology, their meaning is restricted and precise. Thus the title, "a mystic", might be given in the first instance to a romantic young thing who is addicted to the watching of sunsets from hilltops, in the second case to a psychic who is gifted in, let us say, psychometry, and in the third to one called to a high degree of contemplative prayer and whose life has manifested the graces appropriate to such a calling.

The necessity of some measure of definition is therefore clear. It matters a great deal that words should have a clearly understood meaning to all using them, but the plague of over-precision in definition is that it denies room for manœuvre. There must be a certain flexibility in definition if awkward facts that seem reluctant to fit into a prematurely closed system are not to be distorted.

*The Oxford Dictionary of the Christian Church* defines mysticism as "in general, an immediate knowledge of God attained in this life through personal religious experience. It is primarily a state of prayer and as such admits of various degrees from short and rare Divine 'touches' to the practically permanent union with God in the so-called 'mystic marriage'."[1] This, the definition which comes most easily to a Christian is nevertheless far too narrow for my purposes, just as the restriction of all forms of priesthood to the Church and its clergy blinds rather than illuminates our understanding of this great mystery in creation. And so I shall take a second definition together with the first. They are not the same, but neither are they essentially opposed; rather, they complete and complement each other.

Mysticism is "a particular form of consciousness, out of which arise types of experience, akin to, but not to be confused or equated with, those labelled 'religious', and which results in a special sort of 'spirituality', giving that word a wide connotation, and a predisposition to interrogate and interpret the universe in a particular way."[2] This mystical consciousness widens our perspective tremendously, for mysticism is no more in all cases a narrowly "religious" exercise than priesthood is in all cases a narrowly "religious" function. We may go further and wonder to what extent, if at all, Almighty God is "religious".

The writer of the second definition of mysticism says, "I have regarded it as a tenable hypothesis that this 'mystical consciousness' is, of its nature, in some way an enlargement and extension of rational consciousness, resulting in an enlargement and refinement of perception, and consequently having a noetic quality, so that through it knowledge of the 'real' is gained which could not be gained through rational consciousness."[3] It is this mystical consciousness which brings a man into awareness, in the first instance, of dimensions other than those immediately discernable by the five senses, and which forces him to consider fields that are not "home ground" to his rationality. It is this mystical consciousness in men which compels them to search for a within to things, to remain quite incapable of satisfaction with the

---

[1] *Oxford Dictionary of the Christian Church*, p. 935.
[2] F. C. Happold, *Mysticism, a Study and an Anthology*, Penguin, p. 17.
[3] *Ibid.*

phenomenal existence of objects only, and thus to search constantly for the underlying reality behind them.

This mystical consciousness is manifest in a number of forms, and there are many men and women in whom it is strongly present who seem far removed indeed from the narrow definition of "a mystic" with which the theologians would be happy. Thus the perception found in those artistically gifted is related to the same mystical consciousness. The artist seeks to express, in the medium in which he works, the something behind the current subject upon which he is working.

The artist thus stands between two worlds, manifests the "within" and gives it phenomenal expression in this world. The artist is therefore, in some sense, a priest; at least it may be said that there is a priestly potential about this vocation, but this, and the underlying artistic consciousness, depend heavily upon the integrity of the artist. Popularity is insidious; mere technique may paint pretty pictures, either on canvas, in words or in music, but if there is nothing in the artist to say, then nothing will be said. In any generation, much of the artistic output is dictated by fashion, and much is mere exercise in the chosen medium. By no means may we equate "arty" with "mystic", and yet it remains true that there is often a profound connection between the perception of the artist and that of the mystic. Artistic consciousness and mystical consciousness are often united in a person when they may not be equated in the abstract.

Among the many artists in whom this union may be perceived was the poet, Gerard Manley Hopkins. In an introductory essay to a collection of Hopkins' work, the editor writes; "with a searching vision, which often has to coin or remint words to express itself, Hopkins describes trees, breaking waves, the ribbed glacier, and the distant hill whose contour is like 'a slow tune' he eagerly observes the growth and disintegration of everything from a cloud to a bluebell. But he is mainly interested in all those aspects of a thing which make it distinctive and individual. He is always intent on examining that unified complex of characteristics which constitute 'the outward reflection of the inner nature of a thing'. "[1]

This search for the inner nature of a thing is of the very essence of

[1] W. H. Gardner, ed., *Gerard Manley Hopkins*, Penguin Collection, p. xx.

the artistic vision, but on a different plane it is also of the very essence of the mystical consciousness. It might be said, perhaps, that mystical experience is the revelation to that consciousness of a glimpse of the reality which it seeks—or more profoundly, the reality which it is bidden to seek. It is the mystical consciousness which, in the first instance, provokes man to speculate metaphysically; thus provoked, man is engaged in a profoundly moral activity. Thus, "Hopkins must have felt that he had discovered a new aesthetic or metaphysical principle. As a name for that 'individually distinctive' form (made up of various sense-data) which constitutes the rich and revealing 'oneness' of the natural object, he coined the word inscape; and for that energy of being by which all things are upheld, for that natural (but ultimately supernatural) stress which determines an inscape and keeps it in being —for that he coined the name instress."[1]

When Hopkins died in 1889 a small boy of eight was already beginning to share the same kind of vision, in a highly distinctive and very different way, and to search for the inscape, the within of things. He was also to share membership of the Jesuit order with Hopkins, and the same priesthood—in more senses than one—but his search was wider and deeper, and included the inscape of his own being. Pierre Teilhard de Chardin described how, "I took the lamp and, leaving the zone of everyday occupations and relationships where everything seems clear, I went down into my inmost self, to the deep abyss whence I feel dimly that my power of action emanates. But as I moved further and further away from the conventional certainties by which social life is superficially illuminated, I became aware that I was losing contact with myself. At each step of the descent a new person was disclosed within me of whose name I was no longer sure, and who no longer obeyed me. And when I had to stop my exploration because the path faded from beneath my steps, I found a bottomless abyss at my feet, and out of it came—arising I know not from where—the current which I dare to call my life."[2]

Seeking the within of an object is one thing, seeking the within of ones own self is another; and yet it is of the essence of rationality that

---

[1] W. H. Gardner, ed., *op. cit.*, p. xx.
[2] Teilhard de Chardin, *Le Mileu Divin*, pp. 54–5.

it can do just this. But the plumbing of depths—and particularly, the plumbing of ones own depths—can result in the discovery of much more than we bargained for. We can encounter many things, including the unknown—and a very disturbing unknown at that.

Thus Teilhard, returning to the comfortable surroundings of familiar things, found that he was no longer alone. "But then, beneath this very spectacle of the turmoil of life, there reappeared, before my newly-opened eyes, the unknown that I wanted to escape. This time it was not hiding at the bottom of an abyss; it disguised its presence in the innumerable strands which form the web of chance, the very stuff of which the universe and my own small individuality are woven. Yet it was the same mystery without a doubt; I recognised it."[1]

The mystical consciousness is involved in the essentials of all three activities, mysticism, morals (or ethics) and metaphysics. So easily they may become separated and reduced to barren, academic isolation, but they belong together and must remain in touch if they are not to distort and lose their proper balance. Their relationship in man is, roughly, as follows: the mystical consciousness seeks and occasionally encounters: from the encounter two things emerge, the first is an ethical response and the second is an attempt to construct a metaphysical hypothesis which shows the context of things, and helps the reason to come to terms with that which transcends reason.

Hopkins brought into rationality his mystical perception, and evolved a metaphysic of inscapes and instresses. Teilhard de Chardin, with a greater depth of vision, saw the whole of the within of things as a process, a becoming, the evolution of the consciousness of creation in man, the realisation of the potential inherent in all things, and their moving towards their fulfilment, their end product, which he termed the omega point.

The mystical consciousness perceives, and yet it can give very little in the way of an account of itself as to how or why it perceives. Its perceptions are "given", and perhaps the best and the wisest reply that it can give to the question, "where did you learn this?" is that

[1] Teilhard de Chardin, *op. cit.*, pp. 54-5.

offered by the Chinese mystic Chuangtse (d. 275 B.C.), who replied: "I learned it from the Son of Ink, and the Son of Ink learned it from the Grandson of Learning, the Grandson of Learning from Understanding, and Understanding from Insight. Insight learned it from Practice, Practice from Folk Song, and Folk Song from Silence, Silence from the Void, and the Void learned it from the . . . Beginning."[1]

[1] Lin Yutang, *The Wisdom of China*, p. 111.

# 3

# Spirit and Matter

We now find ourselves in search of a principle, yet without being altogether clear what it is; but Hinduism knows what it is, and also has a name for it. The name is *Maya*.

Hinduism is a splendidly syncretistic affair, untroubled either by creeds or by formularies, and the precise interpretation of much of its terminology varies with the interpreter. Terms such as Maya may be used by those whose views are apparently diametrically opposed, although there is a generally agreed understanding as to what it refers.

It is necessary so to stress the looseness of Hindu interpretation because the Western mind is so very different from the Eastern. It is profoundly misleading to take at face value the common English rendering of Maya as "illusion". An illusion, to most of us, is something of a fraud. An illusionist is another name for a conjurer, and while we know him to be a very clever and entertaining fraud, we do not believe in the truth of the tricks that he performs. An illusion is "something that isn't there" in the sense of deceitfulness, and often despair. A mirage is a particularly cruel type of illusion; Maya, as commonly rendered in English, is a mirage. But in fact the word means nothing of the kind; to translate Maya as illusion is to get the whole idea of Maya absolutely wrong.

If we say of this world that it is Maya, and if by that we mean that it is a mere illusion, a mirage-like unreality, then we shall fall into two serious errors; the first is that of world-rejection, the second is the confusion of Maya with a state of affairs. Maya is not a state of affairs so much as a relationship. Maya is also a dynamic principle. Maya has to do with the relationship between this phenomenal world, the material world of the senses, and what we may describe as the within of things; the "world-soul" that Plato and others spoke of, or what the Hindus call the *Brahman*.

To take an illustration, I am sitting in the Rectory garden; its Victorian magnificence is both mellowed and a trifle disordered by the passage of time. It is Springtime and birds are singing in every tree; the blossom is out, the incomparable scent of new-mown grass is in the air, and the hugely overgrown laurels are muffling the traffic noises from the main road. A train clatters past at the far end of the parish, and my daughter's scales and arpeggios issue determinedly from a stone mullioned window. I am tempted to think that this is an archetypal English Rectory idyll. Snowdrop, that most feminine of cats, settles upon my spare typing paper and begins her toilette.

Everything is so solid, so vital, so real. The great, high-romantic, Gothic Rectory, built to last a thousand years, sits four-square in the midst of its lawns. The towering Wellingtonias are rooted, massive, immovable. The graceful spire soars, from the church tower, two hundred feet into a blue sky. The earth feels as though it is the very ground of all being itself. It requires a very real effort of mind and will to bring into consciousness, and formally to acknowledge that fact which every schoolboy knows—that all this, indeed that everything, is but an unimaginable complex of electrical charges, and that every atom in creation is, in Eddington's words, but "the structure of a set of operations".

If I try to translate the intellectual vision into the realm of optics, and naïvely imagine myself possessed of eyes more powerful by far than any microscope, the resulting vision is too awful to contemplate. As I focus upon every object in turn—the house, a tree, the cat, my own right hand—it vanishes, indeed it disintegrates, into a microcosm of the night sky; an immense complex of stars and nebulae hanging in seemingly infinite space. And to my awestruck vision, no vestige of purpose or of order is in the slightest degree immediately discernible.

If this is altogether too daunting an exercise, and I alter my focus somewhat, what must my reaction be upon looking at my own right hand only to discover a whole world of autonomous living cells, being born, dying and being replaced perpetually, and all within the context of what I am pleased to call *my* hand? If this is too much for me, and I shut my eyes, might I not still remember (if my schoolboy memory holds good) that rather more than threequarters of me consists of water? Twist and turn as I may, the same dread question stares me in the face: what am *I*? What and where is that essential something which I call *me*? What is the relationship between the "essential me"—the within of me (which the Hindus call *Atman*) and this physical being of senses, the "phenomenal me" with which I am identified? What is this relationship between the two "me's"? The answer is Maya; but if this most subtle of words is only allowed to mean "illusion" in the sense of a mirage, then I am dangerously near to despair, and the false-mysticism of despair known as "world-rejection".

It must not be forgotten that, in every generation, a great many very thoughtful men and women have taken the view that this phenomenal world is illusory to the point of being evil. In extreme cases they have identified the very concept of matter with evil. This philosophy of despair is in radical opposition to everything the Christian faith stands for—Christians are, or should be, the most truly materialistic of men—but the Church has ever been a prey to world-rejecting influences, especially in the West. Manichaeism and Puritanism in their turn have manifested an incipient rejection of all things "physical" to this day.

World-rejection is an error, and it matters little whether the particular label tied to it is Eastern or Western, ancient or modern. World-rejection implies a total abdication of all human priesthood, but it is the priestly eye of man which perceives that such a relationship exists, that there are—in a sense—two worlds within the created order, and it is the mystical consciousness of man, the priest, which places him between them.

Plato perceived that there is something less than final, less than fully real about the phenomenal world, but in no sense whatever did he reject it. He began with a deep concern for ethics, but as ethics cannot have any meaning in isolation, he found himself evolving a metaphysic of which the ethics were an expression. Some scholars have suggested that Plato's conception was based upon mystical experience, and so the three-fold pattern of mystical experience, moral response and metaphysical speculation is observable here. He contrasted the world of senses and of everyday experience with a kind of heavenly archetype, a world of perfect "Forms", or "Ideas". "The ascent of the soul to the vision of divine Reality, which Plato calls 'the Good', is possible because of the essential nature of the soul. The Good is itself the highest of the Ideas or Forms—the eternal essences or ideal archetypes of things, which constitute the sphere of Reality."[1] "The soul belongs in its inmost nature to the world of Forms. Before its descent into the body, as Plato maintains in *Phaedo* and *Phaedrus*, it existed in the higher world, where it enjoyed an immediate vision of Reality."[2] The concept, familiar to psychology, of the "superego" is a very Platonic one; the soul, in its search for self-realisation, aspires to the perfect good which it perceives, but does not possess.

"The creation of the world in time and space is the main theme of the *Timaeus*. The Creator is the Demiurge (the 'Craftsman'), who makes the world on the model of the eternal order. It has been suggested that the Demiurge, who is also described as God, is the Good considered in its aspect as Creator (through the Forms) of the material universe. . . . In the *Laws*, where Plato deals with the proof of God and the problems of divine providence and human destiny, he thinks of God as the World-Soul—the Source of all movement and change—whereas in the *Timaeus* the World-Soul is the creation of the Demiurge."[3]

Cornford has suggested that "The Forms . . . are 'group-souls' related to the things which participate in their nature as the deity of a mystery-cult, like Dionysus, is related to his group of worshippers. Just as the worshippers of Dionysus believed that in their orgiastic rites 'the one god entered into each and all of them', and they 'partook' of the one divine nature, which was 'communicated' to them all and 'present' in each, so Plato held that the nature of the eternal forms was communicated to, and present in, the objects which resembled them."[4]

---

[1] S. Spencer, *Mysticism in World Religions*, p. 128.
[2] *Ibid.*, p. 129.      [3] *Ibid.*, p. 133.
[4] Cornford, *From Religion to Philosophy*, p. 254. (Quoted Spencer, p. 130.)

The heavenly archetype, the world of forms, is conceived as being the "thoughts of God", and time itself is expounded in a famous expression as "a moving image of eternity". Thus my Rectory and its garden, the traffic in the road, my daughter, my cat and myself are imperfect images, in a world of "becoming", of the perfect archetypes of ourselves in heaven; and my immortal soul, and that of my daughter, —as "seer of eternal truth"—is reminded by the sight of beauty in the phenomenal world, of that eternal Beauty to which it belongs.

Plato was far too great a thinker to be pettifoggingly consistent. His doctrine of God was deficient in that he was without the Revelation which alone could inform and complete it, but Plato's impact upon Christian thought has been profound, and its "metaphysical dualism" is strongly apparent in the Fourth Gospel, as we shall see on a later page. The Incarnation bridged the gulf between the phenomenal world and the archetypal; in the Fourth Gospel, redemption is metaphysical before it is moral. The phenomenal world may, in the Christian belief, be distorted by original sin and "fallen", but the Platonic vision leaves no room whatever for its rejection. In Plato, the priestly function of man is made very plain, although Plato did not use such terms. Man stands between the worlds; they meet in him but he is partly estranged from both.

If Maya is taken to mean "illusion" then it might perhaps describe the imperfect phenomenal world in the Platonic world-view, but at the cost of doing some violence to Plato's own subtlety and sensitivity. But such a description will not fit. Maya refers to a relationship, and Maya is the relationship between the phenomenal world and its own within.

The phenomenal world, the structure of which is known better by us than it ever was by Plato, represents the expression of a divine intention. When we make that effort of mind and will, and recognise that nothing—not even our own selves—is absolute, and that all things are held in being by an eternal will, we are reminded that phenomenal creation, even when fallen, has an integrity of its own and, as Julian of Norwich tells us, "It lasteth, and ever shall last for that God loveth it."

Since Maya is a Hindu term it should be sought in the Upanishads, remembering that Brahman is the world-soul, the within of creation as a whole, and Atman is the individual human soul, the within of man.

The Katha Upanishad[1] says:

"Know the Atman as Lord of a chariot; and the body as the chariot itself.

Know that reason is the charioteer; and the mind indeed is the reins."

The Svetasvatara Upanishad says:

"There is ONE in whose hands is the net of Maya, who rules with his power, who rules all the worlds with his power. He is the same at the time of creation and at the time of dissolution. Those who know him attain immortality. He is Rudra, he alone is the ONE who governs the worlds with his power. He watches over all beings and rules over their creation and their destruction."

Rudra is the Vedic storm god who, like all Hindu deities, is understood as a manifestation of the one God. The Upanishad continues "With Maya, his power of wonder, he made all things, and by Maya the human soul is bound. Know therefore that nature is Maya, but that God is the ruler of Maya; and that all beings in our universe are parts of his infinite splendour."

We discover that Maya is the principle for which we seek; that which causes spirit to find expression in matter, which clothes the essential within of things with phenomenal existence or—if magical terms are preferred—which causes force to be embodied in form. Thus, in the quotation from the Katha Upanishad, Maya is that which gives phenomenal expression to the Atman. As I sit in my Rectory garden, as Snowdrop the cat completes her toilette, as the traffic rumbles past beyond the laurels and as my daughter returns to her scales and her arpeggios, it is Maya which holds together every electron, every atom, every molecule and every cell to give everything that exists its being in the phenomenal world in which we live. Maya is a vital and dynamic principle within the creating and sustaining love of God.

[1] All quotations from Vedas, Upanishads and the Gita from the translations by J. Mascaro published in *Lamps of Fire* and in Penguin editions of the Upanishads and the Bhagavad Gita.

B

# 4

# The "Static Within"

A century and a half before the birth of Plato, the theologians of the Hebrew Exile were at work editing and tidying the various sources which, in their hands, came together to form the Pentateuch, the bed-rock of the Hebrew faith. During this long period of editorial activity the Pentateuch was provided with a theological statement, setting the stage for all that was to follow, which began with these words:

"In the beginning God created the heavens and the earth." (*Gen i. 1*)

At the very beginning of the written record of Revelation, therefore, the doctrine is established of the one God, the eternal, personal Creator, and his creation which is something other than himself and existing in obedience to his will that it should exist. Indeed, the otherness extends, we might say, to two orders of being; to both "the heavens" and the earth; they are not the same, they are separate either from the other. Both are created, neither are to be identified with the Godhead himself.

The whole of Holy Scripture remains consistent with such a vision of God in relation to his creation, and Revelation gradually unfolds, culminating in the Incarnation of our Lord Jesus Christ. The Hebrews have been described as metaphysically naïve, and no doubt they were, but metaphysics was not to be their contribution to the glory of God as revealed to men; theirs was a far higher calling altogether. The Biblical metaphysic, minimal but quite sufficient, is established in the very first sentence of the Bible.

The terms which I have introduced, however, owe their origins to a tradition very different indeed from the Old Testament; it is necessary, therefore, to delve a little deeper into their background and to do some searching of the Hindu scriptures in the process, superficial though this must be. But first it is very necessary to be quite clear about the difference of approach between the Western mind and the Eastern, and between the Christian mind and the Hindu.

To the Christian, confident assertions, based upon Revelation, and tightly circumscribed creeds and formularies, are not only possible, they seem to be both natural and necessary. For Christians are united by a common belief, in the first place, and by a common relationship, both with each other and with God in the second place. Christians accept by faith a series of facts about God, as revealed by Jesus the Christ, the Eternal Son of God, to whom their love and their devotion is to be wholly and freely given. The Christian Revelation is of a person, who is both God and man, and in whom God and man are reconciled and made one.

Christians are bound to proclaim the Truth revealed, and at the same time they are bound to preserve it from half-truth and perversion by formulating definitive creeds and dogmas. It is natural, therefore, for the Christian to project a similar precision upon the Hindu religious tradition which he may take it upon himself to study; and in the Western European Christian, this tendency to project order and tidy-mindedness will be extreme. The Christian is almost bound to imagine that Hindu scripture is consistent, and that there is a credal and dog-matic structure to Hinduism. But if he does so imagine, then he is in error; there is nothing of the kind.

The word *Dharma* is commonly taken to mean "religion" in the Western understanding of that word. It is far better translated as "way of life" or even "civilisation". It has been translated as "national righteousness", and has much more to do with the nature of man, and his behaviour, than it has to do with his beliefs. "While it gives abso-lute liberty in the world of thought, it enjoins a strict code of practice. The theist and the atheist, the sceptic and the agnostic may all be Hindus if they accept the Hindu system of culture and life . . . what counts is conduct, not belief."[1] It follows, therefore, that Hinduism is

[1] Radhakrishnan, *The Hindu View of Life.*

not a religion at all as Christians would understand religion; it is a Dharma.

The most important of the Hindu scriptures may be divided into two sections which, taken together, are roughly contemporary with the Old Testament. The Vedas, which as Max Müller claims are "the first word spoken by Aryan man," date from perhaps 1500 B.C. to 800 B.C. Some authorities would date them much earlier. The Upanishads, more sophisticated by far than the Vedas, and more metaphysical in content, span the five hundred years or so from 800 B.C. onward. Thus the Vedas may be roughly dated with the Pentateuchal sources, and the Upanishads with the Prophets. The sacred writings did not stop with the great Upanishads, but the canon of Hindu scripture is a loose one and undefined.

The greatest of the Vedas is the Rigveda, roughly contemporary with the first and second book of Samuel in the Old Testament and with the Kingship of David. In Mascaro's fine translation, the Rigveda has this to say of "the Beginning":

"There was not then what is nor what is not. There was no sky, and no heaven beyond the sky. What power was there? Where? Who was that power? Was there an abyss of fathomless waters?

There was neither death or immortality then. No signs were there of night or day. The ONE was breathing by its own power, in infinite peace. Only the ONE was: there was nothing beyond.

Darkness was hidden in darkness. The all was fluid and formless. Therein, in the void, by the fire of fervour arose the ONE.

And in the ONE arose love. Love the first seed of soul. The truth of this the sages found in their hearts: seeking in their hearts with wisdom, the sages found that bond of union between being and non-being.

Who knows in truth? Who can tell whence and how arose this universe? The gods are later than its beginning: who knows therefore whence comes this creation?

Only that god who sees in highest heaven: he only knows whence comes this universe, and whether it was made or uncreated. He only knows, or perhaps he knows not."

"The gods are later than its beginning" is a significant phrase for, as in the Greek pantheon (and all others) the gods are archetypal entities representing aspects of Reality but not the whole of it. They are Plato's "forms", embodied virtues and principles, but they are not in themselves what a Christian means when he speaks of God. There is, however, a difference between the gods and God in Hindu thought. And the various deities are identified with each other in various traditions.

"Behold the universe in the glory of God: and all that lives and moves on earth"

says the Isa Upanishad. The Prasna Upanishad tells us:

"In the beginning, the Creator longed for the joy of creation. He remained in meditation, and then came *Rayi*, matter, and *Prana*, life. 'These two,' thought he, 'will produce beings for me.' "

The Chandogya Upanishad asks "Wherefrom do all these worlds come?" and answers,

"They come from space. All beings arise from space, and into space they return: space is indeed their beginning, and space is their final end."

It is clear that there is a great difference in style and concern between the Bible and both the Rigveda and the Upanishads. The latter are more philosophical; they contain great mystical insight and profound speculation, and they compliment the Old Testament profoundly. But they lack the assurance of divine Revelation for which they endlessly seek.

The Upanishads talk of *purusha* and *prakriti*, "spirit" and "matter" respectively. But there is as much imprecision about the use of the word purusha as there is in English about the use of the word "spirit". The word can mean "spirit" in the abstract, it can mean an eternal entity of consciousness, generally understood as the human soul, or, as in the Katha Upanishad, it can refer to the "world-soul", *and* to the Creator:

"Beyond the Spirit in man is the Spirit of the universe, and beyond is Purusha, the Spirit Supreme. Nothing is beyond Purusha: He is the End of the path."

There is no precision in Hindu theology. The Hindu is generally considered to be a monist and to regard all creation as being identified in some way with the Creator and in some sense "part" of him. The Katha Upanishad, which at one point distinguishes between God and creation (as above), at another point seems to identify the two:

"Even by the mind this truth is to be learned: there are not many but only ONE. Who sees the many and not the ONE wanders on from death to death. . . .

There is one Ruler, the Spirit that is in all things, who transforms his one form into many. Only the wise who see him in their souls attain the peace eternal.

'That is that,' thus they feel the ineffable joy supreme."

The identification of all things with the ONE is found in the Mandukya Upanished, in which the word *Om*, meaning "the Yes" to all things is expounded:

"OM. This eternal Word is all: what was, what is, what shall be, and what beyond is in Eternity. All is OM. Brahman is all, and Atman is Brahman. Atman, the Self, the Spirit in man has four conditions. . . .

This (fourth condition of) Atman is the eternal Word OM. This Word has three sounds: A and U—these two are O—and M. These three sounds are the first three states of consciousness.

The Word OM as one sound is the fourth state of supreme consciousness. It is beyond the senses: it is beyond sound. It is love."

The Chandogya Upanishad implies the essential priesthood of man —but without using these terms—when it proclaims:

"There is a bridge between time and Eternity; and this bridge is Atman, the Spirit in man."

The nature of God is unclear to the Hindu, but there is a generally accepted doctrine of the Trinity, different though it is from that given in the Christian revelation. Of the three persons of the Hindu Trinity, *Brahma* is "Creator" (*Prajapati*, "Lord of offspring"), *Vishnu* is the "Preserver" and *Siva* (*Nataraja*, "Lord of the dance") is the "Destroyer-

and-re-Creator". Often, *Brahma* is equated with *Brahman*, the "world-soul", the within of the totality of creation, but this is by no means always the case; the Mundaka Upanishad begins with the words:

> "Brahma was before the gods were, the Creator of all, the Guardian of the Universe. The vision of Brahman, the foundation of all wisdom, he gave in revelation to his first-born son Atharvan."

The Chandogya Upanishad underlines this otherness of the Creator:

> "Prajapati (that is to say Brahma), the Creator of all, rested in life-giving meditation over the worlds of his creation."

And the Katha Upanishad confuses what might seem to be doctrinal clarity with its beautiful hymn:

> "The Tree of Eternity has its roots in heaven above and its branches reach down to earth. It is Brahman, pure Spirit, who in truth is called the Immortal. All the worlds rest on that Spirit and beyond him no one can go: This in truth is That.
>
> The whole universe comes from him and his life burns through the whole universe. In his power is the majesty of thunder. Those who know him have found immortality."

There is no doctrinal consistency in Hindu scripture. There is no attempt at any such thing because these writings are the writings of schools of poets and mystics who sought to express the insights of mystical experience and to build some kind of metaphysic upon them. But the Eastern mind is less concerned with tidy, rationalistic systems than the Western and so the Hindu metaphysic is looser and less systematised than the Greek. The Eastern mind accepts otherness for what it is and makes no attempt to define a mystery. This is the difference between the minds of East and West. But we are Westerners (or at least the writer is), and so let us analyse what we can from what we have read.

There is a doctrine of God the Creator, the Sustainer and the re-Creator. There is evidence to suppose a doctrine of creation as seen to be other than the Creator. But at the same time there is great evidence to support the identification of creation with the Creator, and it is this latter which constitutes the most generally accepted theology of Hinduism, as an ism.

There is also a clear understanding about the expression of the within of things in phenomenal form, and also the corollary to this, that the phenomenal world has a within of which it is the outward expression. The within of the totality of things is called Brahman. The within of the human soul—the human "true, or higher self"—is called Atman. "Matter" is the phenomenal expression of the underlying "spirit" and Maya is the dynamic principle by which this expression is made.

Does the general ethos of Hindu scripture permit us to construct such a statement as that which begins the Old Testament? Can we extract, "In the beginning, God created the heavens and the earth" from the Upanishads? It is uncertain that we could. It would be easier to find, let us say, "in the beginning, God created earth", understanding by "earth" the within and its phenomenal expression.

The hereafter, in Hindu thought, is confined to the totality of the created order, and it is this that is rather vaguely identified with divinity. The work of the Yogi is that of uniting his Atman with the Brahman thus ending the round of incarnation and reincarnation. The Svetasvatara Upanishad proclaims:

> "When a man knows God, he is free: his sorrows have an end, and birth and death are no more. When in inner union he is beyond the world of the body, then the third world, the world of the Spirit is found, where the power of the All is, and man has all: for he is one with the ONE."

"The wandering swan of the soul" seeks rest in God, be the soul Christian or Hindu. By no means do the Upanishads deny the reality of heaven, but the within of the phenomenal universe is not readily distinguishable from a clear idea of a heavenly state which is truly other, just as there is no clear distinction of the Creator with creation. Hinduism can only speculate, on the basis of the collective experience of its mystics, who are many; like every other pre-Christian religious system, heaven is confused with and sometimes identified with what

the occult world calls "the inner planes". Spirituality cannot readily
be disentangled from psychism.

It is very probable that a naïve view of astronomy made its contribution to the Hebrew metaphysic which was proclaimed in the opening
sentence of Holy Scripture. God, in the beginning, created "the
heavens" and the earth. But metaphysically naïve though the priest-
editors may have been (and we cannot be sure that they were), they
found themselves in substantial agreement with Plato who was clear
about a creation on two planes. The distinction between the within
of the lower and the world of Forms he also considered. In the light
of the Upanishads it seems no longer certain that there is a distinction
between the within of creation and that state of perfection and fulfilment with Christ in God which we call "heaven" and which Plato
dimly perceived as the world of perfect Ideas or Forms? It may equally
be asked if there is a distinction between psychism and spirituality? It
is better to suspend judgement at this stage.

# 5

# The "Dynamic Within"

The question of the essential difference between the Old Testament and the Vedas and Upanishads is a very big one indeed, but if one, very general, answer were to be advanced it would probably be as follows: That the Old Testament is the record of a process, the working out of Revelation in the course of human history, culminating in a climactic, historical event of absolute importance for the whole of creation; the Hindu sacred writings, however, are devoid of any sense of process and manifest no awareness of the deep significance of human history. The Old Testament is dynamic, the Hindu scriptures are static.

Staticism is an ever-present temptation to the Church. One of the doctrines of the Western Church, once proclaimed and now quietly forgotten, was that of the "Fixity of Species". It held to a wholly pre-scientific view of creation and drew its authority from a literal interpretation of the first chapter of Genesis. The book of Genesis was not, however, intended to be referred to as a scientific text-book, or even as a statement of biological history. It is theology, and in parts "theological poetry". Indeed the very idea of "fixity" is utterly foreign to the whole spirit of those Scriptures quoted in support of it. It belongs more truly to the world of the Upanishads than to that of the Bible.

Inevitably, both sets of Scriptures are man-centred, but in different ways. The Hindu scriptures are concerned almost exclusively with man; the rest of phenomenal creation is but a stage upon which man must, ideally, perform his *yoga*, his work of seeking the total and final identification of his Atman with the Brahman, and so being relieved at last of the round of successive incarnations. The relationship between man and the world he inhabits—with his fellow-creatures—is not a matter of great concern; man has enough to do coping with himself.

The Old Testament is utterly different in character; man is indeed central, but he is seen as being set very firmly in a prepared context and standing in a defined relationship with his Creator on the one hand, and the rest of creation on the other. The Bible proclaims the intrinsic worth of creation in its very first chapter. The priest-editors of Genesis, in their Exile, understood creation as being deliberate, specific and in an ascending order of being. God, in creating it, "saw that it was good" (*Gen 1:12*) and having brought beings into creation in a rational order, God created man "in our own image, in the likeness of ourselves" (*Gen 1:26*) and gave him clear orders:

> "Be fruitful, multiply, fill the earth and conquer it. Be masters of the fish of the sea, the birds of heaven and all living animals on the earth." (*Gen 1:28*)

Man has his place within God's creation as God's manager, as the objectively and morally conscious being through whom God rules over creation. This is a doctrine of man which is of astonishing exaltation, and it is stated at the very beginning of the Bible. Man is God's priest, he stands between God and creation, himself a creature. To be more accurate, he stands between the perfect "world of Ideas or Forms" which we call "heaven", and this imperfect world which we call "earth" or the Cosmos. His priesthood is potential rather than actual, it is yet to be fully realised, it is not yet fulfilled in the Pentateuchal understanding. The priesthood has little to do with "the practice of religion" as this is—far too narrowly—defined; it is fundamental to man's being, and indeed it is the reason for his being.

The unfolding of Revelation, from Genesis thereafter, is the record of a very deliberate process, the process of fulfilment of the priesthood of man in the person of the Christ. The Vedas and the Upanishads, however, proclaims no essential role for man to grow into and fulfil; man, as a species, just simply is.

The lack of any sense of history or of process in the Hindu sacred writings is linked with another shortcoming. Like the Old Testament, they were written by men innocent of any vestige of scientific knowledge. To be sure, primitive and pre-scientific man made remarkable achievements, and even today primitive man performs feats of communication and navigation by psychic means which the instruments of his technological brother merely repeat but with far greater precision and range of operation. Man was, at the time of these writings, closer by far to his instinct-motivated animal brethren. But whereas the Revelation begun in the Old Testament and fulfilled in the New is unaffected by the discoveries of science, the other scriptures are not so accommodating. The reason is not hard to find. The Holy Bible is concerned with the personal relationship between God and man, and between man and man. The Hindu scriptures, on the other hand, are born of mystical experience and are metaphysical rather than moral in their concerns. Metaphysics is an academic exercise and is modified with every fresh understanding of the nature of creation.

The revelations of God the Holy Spirit to man, through the disciplines of science, have, in the last century and a half, affected man's metaphysical understanding profoundly. It is clear that the within of things is a far more complex and many-dimensioned reality than those devout and inspired souls who coined the terms Atman, Brahman and Maya could ever have supposed. The terms, and the concepts that lie behind them, are by no means invalidated, but their scope is widened very substantially and their character is permanently affected.

It has been the lot of a number of thinkers, of whom Teilhard de Chardin is perhaps the most prominent, to perceive with a new clarity the essential process of things, and to discover the whole process of evolution, as perceived by science, to be the manner (or part at any rate of the manner) by which God brings his creation to its final plenitude. The impact upon Christian thought has been tremendous, but prophetic vision is so often "a blinding glimpse of the obvious", as someone put it, that it is difficult, after a little while, to imagine a time when this vision was not a commonplace. So it is, essentially, in the case of the thoroughly dynamic vision of Teilhard which is most fully expounded in his great work, *The Phenomenon of Man*. He is concerned, at the outset, to proclaim the within of things, and explains: "When I speak of the 'within' of the earth, I do not of course mean those material depths in which—only a few miles beneath our feet—lurks one of the most vexatious mysteries of science: the chemical nature and the exact physical condition of the internal regions of the globe. The 'within' is used here, . . . to denote the 'psychic' face of that portion of the stuff of the cosmos enclosed from the beginning of time within the narrow scope of the earthly earth. In that fragment of sidereal matter which has just been isolated, as in every other part of the universe, the exterior world must inevitably be lined at every point with an interior one."[1]

Teilhard's canvas is as wide as the universe. Of the origins of matter itself he says little; it is fairly commonplace in scientific circles that hydrogen atoms, the smallest of all, seem to come into existence *ex nihilo* in inter-galactic space. The cohesion of such atoms into gas clouds and the emergence from such clouds of galaxies of hundreds of millions of stars are matters about which scientists can argue to an almost limitless extent. Our minds cannot contain the images that such processes suggest, and the mere arithmetic is so vast as to become meaningless. Teilhard is content to take such processes for granted and to concentrate his attentions upon our own earth, for "it is *the only place* in the world in which we are so far able to study the evolution of matter in its ultimate phases, and as far as ourselves."[2]

Teilhard's vision is of the purposeful evolution of the whole of the created order, centred upon man, in whom the consciousness inherent in creation is realised. "In such a vision," he maintains, "man is seen not as a static centre of the world—as he for long believed himself to be—but as the axis and leading shoot of evolution, which is something much finer."[3]

"What arouses the physicists's interest in this globe—new-born, it would seem, by a stroke of chance in the cosmic mass—is the presence of composite chemical bodies not to be observed anywhere else. At the extreme temperatures occurring in the stars, matter can only

[1] Teilhard de Chardin, *The Phenomenon of Man*, pp. 71-2.
[2] *Ibid.*, p. 67.
[3] *Ibid.*, p. 36.

survive in its most dissociated states. On the earth this simplicity of the elements still obtains at the periphery, in the more or less ionised gases of the atmosphere and the stratosphere and, probably, far below in the metals of the 'barysphere.' But between these two extremes comes a long series of complex substances, harboured and produced only by stars that have 'gone out'. Arranged in successive zones, they demonstrate from the start the powers of synthesis contained in the universe. First the siliceous zone, preparing the solid crust of the planet. Next the zone of water and carbonic acid, enclosing the silicates in an unstable, mobile and penetrating envelope. In other words we have the barysphere, lithosphere, hydrosphere, atmosphere and stratosphere."[1]

Teilhard enlarges upon his theme, and takes note of the properties and the behaviour of matter. "In the course of and by virtue of the initial advance of the elements on earth towards the crystalline state, energy was constantly released and liberated (just as, today, it is released by mankind as a result of machinery). This was constantly augmented by energy furnished by the atomic decomposition of radio-active substances and by that given off by solar rays. Where could this surplus energy, available on the surface of the earth in its early stages, go to? Was it merely to be lost around the globe in obscure emanations?"

"Another much more probable hypothesis occurs to us when we look at the world today. When it became too weak to escape in incandescence, the free energy of the new-born earth was compensated by the power of reacting on itself in a work of synthesis. Thus, as today, it passed with the absorption of heat into building up certain carbonates, hydrates or hydrites, and nitrates like those which astonish us by their power to increase indefinitely the complexity and instability of their elements. This is the realm of *polymerisation*, in which the particles 'concatenate' and group themselves, as in crystals, in a theoretically endless network. *Only, this time it is molecules with molecules in such a way as to form on each occasion (by closed or at all events limited combination) an ever larger and more complex molecule.* This world of 'organic compounds' is ours. We live among them and are made of them. . . . There is good reason to think that around our nascent

[1] Teilhard de Chardin, *The Phenomenon of Man*, p. 68.

planet, in addition to the incohation of a metallic barysphere, a siliceous lithosphere, a hydrosphere and an atmosphere, there was the outline of a special envelope, the antithesis, we might say, of the first four: the temperate zone of polymerisation, in which water, ammonia and carbon dioxide were already floating in the rays of the sun. To ignore that tenuous film would be to deprive the infant earth of its most essential adornment. For, as we shall see, it is in this that the *'within'* of the earth was soon to be gradually concentrated."[1]

Teilhard's vision is eminently Biblical; the above is essentially the restatement of the first dozen or so verses of the first chapter of Genesis. The restatement of the remainder occupies a hundred pages during which Teilhard outlines the development of a biosphere of living organisms which in turn evolves Man, and in man the noosphere, a collective all-conscious, the inexorably unifying principle by which God "would bring everything together under Christ, as head, everything in the heavens and everything on earth" (*Eph 1:10*). The Church is thus Omega, "already in existence and operative at the very core of the thinking mass".[2] But the dynamic within of Teilhard's vision is not quite the same as the essentially static within of the Upanishads. And it will not do to merely oppose the two concepts, and choose one while rejecting the other. There is no "either–or" choice, it is a matter of "both-and", for the static and the dynamic are not by any means opposed, they are essentially complementary and must be firmly grasped and held together as such.

There is, however, one very close—and quite unexpected—similarity between the Upanishadic concept of the within and that of the scientific mysticism of Teilhard de Chardin. Both seem to tend towards a modification of that first sentence of Genesis; both seem to imply, "In the beginning, God created the earth!" Teilhard's vision was essentially, and very properly, earthbound. It was to be his contribution to enlarge the vision of man in respect of the purposes of God in this imperfect Cosmos, to point to the coming fulfilment of the phenomenal world and its own dynamic within. Of "heaven" in any of its images—the plane of pure Forms, the archetypal perfect world, a state

---

[1] *Ibid.*, pp. 70–1.
[2] *Ibid.*, p. 291.

of being with a dynamic relationship with that order of creation of which we are a part—of anything like this he says little or nothing, and it was not his mission to do so. As an orthodox Christian he would be the first to repudiate any such modification of the first verse of Genesis as I have suggested; but it may be doubted if the correct version could very easily be constructed from a study of his own works.

Teilhard was vitally concerned with eschatology and had something at least of a glimpse of the Parousia, but of heaven as a present dynamic, as opposed to the within of the Cosmos, he says no more than that which is implied in the quotation already given, of the Church as Omega "already in existence and operative" within the created order.

All the foregoing has been, to a very large extent, concerned exclusively with man. Man's place in the world, man's evolution, man's future, man's function, man's relationship with his Creator—these mighty matters, of incalculable import, and at the heart of all our thinking, can very easily blind us to the fact that man's concerns have two directions in which to face, both of them outward.

The vision of Teilhard de Chardin is of man, the ultimately emergent mind and mouthpiece of creation; the creature through whom the Creator enters into a personal relationship with creation as a whole. This vision reminds us that, in respect of all of his creation, "God saw that it was good," and also that man is placed in authority over it. Man, we have said, is God's manager. So he is, but he is more than this, he is God's priest. Priesthood carries with it authority to bear rule, in specific matters, over those to whom the priesthood is exercised. Man's is a "managerial priesthood" or, as the commoner phrase puts it, a ministerial priesthood.

In the affairs of men, the manager's concern is twofold. He is very concerned for his relationship with his employer, but this relationship very largely depends upon the quality of his relationship with his subordinates. Indeed, the more he attends to his duties, the better he cares for the persons and goods over which he is set, the better he serves his employer. The manager will not long hold down his job who neglects his employer's affairs in order to indulge in fawning adulation of the boss! The manager stands between two worlds, partaking in some measure of both (but the lower in particular) and at the same time isolated from both, bearing the pain and the loneliness of his position. The perfect manager, in an ideal human situation, is a priest, and all management partakes of the nature of priesthood. In the world of men, the manager may be harried into an early grave in the interests of higher production and increased profits; he will not often be asked "to lay down his life for the sheep"—for the love of them. This is a measure of the "spoiled priesthood" of human management.

Man is both priest and manager, and he must take his position seriously and recognise it for what it is. He is not to be concerned merely with himself, he is to be concerned for his brethren over whom he bears rule. The farmer is priest to his cow.

It is perhaps a little too easy to assume, from the evolutionist enthusiasm of the school of Teilhard de Chardin, that man is all in God's creation, and that the rest of the created order, having produced man— or, by being off-shoots from the main stem, having produced something else—has no more part to play in the scheme of things, and must therefore "pass away". This is a thoroughly unbiblical parody. All things are created "good", which is to say that they have each their own integrity, are loved by God who created them, and are held in being by God in the perpetual exercise of that self-giving love which gives all things their being. God loves them and, as his priests, so must we.

# 6

# Within the Within

"Modern man", in the view of Dr C. G. Jung, "is somehow fascinated by the almost pathological manifestations of the unconscious mind."[1] The concept, empirically arrived at, of the unconscious mind—and even more, of the collective unconscious—introduces a new series of dimensions.

Already the idea of the absolute object has had to be abandoned. Physics, let alone metaphysics, will no longer permit any such concept, and what once seemed to be comfortingly solid matter is already acknowledged to be, in some way, a concentrated form of energy. This much is almost a commonplace. Phenomenal existence knows no absolutes. And further, the concept of absolute time is no more viable than that of absolute matter. The universe can only be described at all satisfactorily as a multi-dimensional space-time continuum; and having thus described the universe, it is virtually impossible to maintain any clear image of what is meant by such a description!

The dilemma that quickly faces anybody who seeks, objectively, to determine just what does constitute that which he calls *me*, is such that it is hard to argue with the suggestion that the conscious part of a man's mind is like the tip of an iceberg, and that the unconscious depths are, at the very least, of considerable extent. Jung argues: "Whoever denies the existence of the unconscious is in fact assuming that our present knowledge of the psyche is total. And this belief is clearly just as false as the assumption that we know all there is to be known about the natural universe. Our psyche is part of nature, and its enigma is limitless. Thus we cannot define the psyche or nature.

---

[1] C. G. Jung, *Modern Man in Search of a Soul*, p. 238.

We can merely state what we believe them to be and describe, as best we can, how they function."[1]

The curious fact is that denials, *a priori*, of the whole field of psycho-therapy—and psycho-analysis in particular—are widespread; indeed they are as widespread as similar denials, *a priori*, of the reality of psychic phenomena, and the reasons are one and the same. Fear of the unknown, fear of dangers lurking within, unconscious fears "lest this should be applicable to me" lead to wholly irrational, point-blank denials of the reality of whole areas of human experience. But this is unmanly evasion, and disquieting possibilities have to be faced if we are to fulfil our very humanity. It will be the aim of the present study to look a number of unmentionable activities squarely in the face, and seek to establish their purpose and their place in the scheme of things; no faith is worth anything that has to resort to evasions, or to deny that which it cannot apparently contain.

The concept of the individual unconscious is one thing, that of the collective unconscious is quite another; and yet the collective researches of Jung and his school led them to the point at which such a hypothesis was inescapable. It has been the experience of psychotherapists, using Jungian disciplines, that the collective unconscious is a reality to be taken for granted. It is not merely that human society, as it were "horizontally", appears to possess a collective heritage of myths and symbolisms such as Frazer enumerates exhaustively in *The Golden Bough*, but rather that society "vertically", in each successive genera-tion, and in its four-dimensional totality (Time being the fourth dimen-sion) is equally heir to a heritage of archetypes, symbols, images and so on.

The human mind is forever looking for pictorial images in which to contain the various concepts presented to it. A naïve pictorial image of the unconscious, both individual and collective, is frogspawn in a pond. The mass of jelly is in fact made up of individual globes of jelly, each with a tiny black dot in the middle. It is as if the jelly is the uncon-scious, both collective and individual, and each tiny black dot is an individual conscious mind. There is a constant "osmosis"—a flow of symbolic material—between the various unconscious minds, impinging

[1] C. G. Jung, *Man and his Symbols*, p. 23.

upon the conscious in various ways. The mass of jelly is of limitless extent—but the mental picture breaks down when we introduce the fourth dimension, Time. It is beyond us to imagine the collective unconscious with our own consciousness after all.

But another dimension is added to the Jungian concept by the vision of Teilhard de Chardin which sees consciousness inherent in the whole of "matter"; not only in primaeval slime, but in the most newly-created hydrogen atom in inter-galactic space. At once the whole concept of the collective unconscious is enlarged and extended beyond words until it extends in every respect to the limits of the Cosmos. This concept is Brahman, the world-soul, the within of the totality of the Cosmos. The static within of the Hindu metaphysics has been discovered to have a dynamic principle after all. And to return to the naïve pictorial image—may not the label Atman be tied to the black dot within each individual globe of unconscious jelly?

Pictorial images no sooner clarify than they begin to bedevil and confuse, and they must be firmly discarded as soon as this happens. But it is probably even more true that semantics bedevil human dialogue as effectively as anything else, and Jung has done a notable service to mankind by providing "neutral" terms for a number of concepts to which different groups of people have applied widely different terminologies. Thus, as we have seen, the concept of the collective unconscious has, with considerable, yet cautious, extensions, thrown much new light upon Hindu terminology and it has effected somewhat of a reconciliation between this and the dynamic concepts of Teilhard de Chardin. It is now relevant to turn briefly to another discipline altogether, the world of occultism.

An overall definition of occultism is exceedingly difficult to arrive at; it covers a huge field of belief, theory and practice and is, to some occultists, an exact science, to others a religious system in its own right, and to others still, a dimension of their own practice as convinced Christians. The classic theology of occultism is monistic, but in a somewhat developed sense. To most occultists, God "manifests" rather than creates. There is a fairly sophisticated doctrine by which God is identified with his creation, and "manifestation" proceeds through various stages of concretion until the point is reached at which force is contained in form in its densest state and the phenomenal world of matter is made manifest.

Classically, man is the microcosm and God is the Macrocosm in occult theology; the great work of man is so to exalt himself that he becomes God. Thus stated, this aim must seem repellant to the Christian and savour of every kind of spiritual pride; but in fact the union of Atman with Brahman is what is meant, for Western occultism has a very great deal in common with Hinduism, both in theology and in some practice.

The occult terminologies are numerous and range from the precise to the almost meaningless. However, the term Astral Plane is common currency, and the Inner Planes in general may be more or less identified with the collective unconscious and the Brahman. Occultism is a Dharma, a general climate of opinion and practice, embracing variations of practice and indeed of aim which are remarkable in their variety. Responsible, "white" occultism is unspectacular and seldom heard about; it ranges from various manifestations of spiritism to the practice of ritual magic. Occult practice varies from healing and intercessory magic to the deliberate penetration, by meditation and enactment of symbolic ritual, of what we would call the collective unconscious, to the end that ever more and more of the within should come into conscious awareness and control, and that, in the end, the occultist should become the All-Conscious. The technical term for all this is magic, and magic is defined as "the art of causing changes in consciousness in accordance with the will." It is a technical term, not a pejorative one, if we would understand it aright. Magic is the technique of deliberately working "within the within". It goes without saying that the dangers and temptations attending a magician are extreme.

The tendency, in classical occultism, is to regard the within of creation as the whole of the "hereafter" and thus to equate what we would call "heaven" with the within of the Cosmos. As the Qabalistic occultists at any rate would understand it, the within has four main "levels", usually known as the four worlds. These are as follows:

*Atziluth*   The archetypal world
*Briah*      The creative world

*Yetzirah*    The formative world
*Assiah*    The material world

The names are Hebrew, and the Qabalah is a metaphysical framework of Jewish origin. The "worlds" represent plains of manifestation, refining from the fourth, Assiah—the phenomenal world of matter—to Atziluth—the archetype of manifestation, from whence all things pass into the "limitless light". The Qabalistic system is profound in so far as it is taken to refer to the within of the Cosmos, but the Qabalist could not say, with the editors of Genesis, "In the beginning God created the heavens and the earth"; he would rather say, "In the beginning of manifestation, when God emanated the various planes." The Cosmos, and the within of the Cosmos, represent the limit of things to the classical occultist.

At this point I am faced with a matter of considerable difficulty which it would be agreeable to avoid; for it is the clear and stated intention of occultists to seek to "become contacted on the inner planes", that is to say, to establish contact with human beings who are no longer on this earth, and to work with them towards a desired end. This, occultists claim to do, and thereafter to work under the guidance or direction of a discarnate human being whose "habitation" or "context" is as they suppose, within the within of the Cosmos.

The great authority on Qabalistic occultism, the late Dion Fortune has this to say of "the Masters" (discarnate guides) with whom she and others worked. "Concerning the 'Masters' or Inner Plane Adepti I should like to make it clear that these are of a far higher stage of development than those discarnate communicators who describe the 'summerlands', personal 'heaven-worlds', etc., of their own subjective Inner-Plane state. The latter have little of value to tell the average well-educated man; the former have a very great deal but usually work only through carefully chosen and highly trained individuals save, of course, for the 'contacts' each of us may succeed in making for himself and which result in intuitional apprehension. This, however, should be treated with great caution and unless the matter given is sound should not be taken as genuine."[1] Dion Fortune gives some

[1] Dion Fortune, *The Cosmic Doctrine*, pp. 7–8.

further descriptions of these inner plane guides in passages she claims to have received verbatim from them concerning themselves: "What are the Masters? Human beings like yourselves, but older. They are not Gods, nor Angels, nor Elementals but are those individuals who have achieved and completed the same task as you have set yourselves. What you are now, they were once. What they are now, you can be. . . . The Masters as you picture them are all 'imagination'. Note well that I did not say that the Masters were imagination; I said, 'The Masters as you picture them'. What we are you cannot realise and it is a waste of time to try to do so but you can imagine us on the astral plane and we can contact you through your imagination, and although your mental picture is not real or actual, the results of it are real and actual."[1]

The mystical consciousness defined at the beginning of this work is by no means to be identified with what may be called psychic consciousness, or better still, the psychic sense. The psychic sense is a primitive faculty which belongs to the time of man's immaturity. As Jung states in a work quoted earlier, "man has developed consciousness slowly and laboriously, in a process that took ages to reach the civilised state (which is arbitrarily dated from the invention of script in about 4000 B.C.). And this evolution is far from complete, for large areas of the human mind are still shrouded in darkness."[2] The psychic sense belongs to that "shrouded" part of the human mind and is strong in some people and weak in others. This sense tends to run strongly in some races and in certain families and informs by intuition rather than by reason. It is in the deliberate exercise of the psychic sense that inner plane contacts are made and mind-to-mind communication established from a discarnate consciousness to an incarnate consciousness. But the means of communication lies below the level of human rationality, and, the incarnate psychic providing the bulk of the energy, the possibility of subjective distortion and error is considerable. By the same mechanism, telepathic communication between two living persons can and frequently does take place, the "link" being established via the collective unconscious. This will be considered in greater detail in the final section of this book.

[1] *Ibid.*, p. 9.     [2] C. G. Jung, *Man and his Symbols*, p. 23.

It will be appreciated by now how very easily psychism may be mistaken for spirituality, and how very vital those words at the beginning of Genesis are. God created heaven and earth. The within of the phenomenal world is not to be equated with heaven. The occultist is being true to his theology and (if he is a 'white' occultist) he may well feel that he is following a vocation for which he is made—God is the judge of this—but his theology is inadequate, and what he often describes as mysticism is in fact magic. To say this is by no means to pass a judgement, it is merely to draw a necessary distinction and to state fact. An identification of God with creation can and indeed always does result in a confusion of magic with mysticism, of psychism with spirituality, and issues in a search for ultimate reality within creation as a whole, whereas, in the Christian understanding, creation is in God.

It is for these reasons that psychism was expressly forbidden in the Old Testament; it had nothing to do with the personal relationship between man and his Maker and could only distort, confuse and pervert the Revelation slowly unfolding. Thus the Hebrews were commanded, "There must never be anyone among you who makes his son or daughter pass through fire, who practices divination, who is a soothsayer, augur or sorcerer, who uses charms, consults ghosts or spirits, or calls up the dead. For the man who does these things is detestable to Yahweh your God." (*Deut 18:10–12.*) This, in the context of the times, when all religion was heavily psychically orientated, is a very remarkable prohibition indeed, but the seriousness with which it was taken is shown by the death penalty specified for anyone who "goes and serves other gods and worships them, or the sun or the moon or any of heaven's array". (*Deut 17:2, 3.*) It was as vital as this to distinguish, in the minds of God's People between creation and its within, its inner planes, and the Creator and his heaven which (however it is to be understood) is wholly "other".

So man, as the first chapter of Genesis sees him, is God's manager, God's steward, God's priest over the phenomenal world; he stands between God and inanimate or inarticulate creation, he is the mind of the Cosmos and its mouthpiece. But the Cosmos is more than it seems to be. What we call "matter" is the phenomenal expression of "spirit", and indeed the phenomenal world of matter and the senses is but a thin crust to a vast within which, in totality, we have come to call Brahman or the "world-soul". Yet the Cosmos is made up of particular things, each with its own integrity, and the within of man, the priest, can be called Atman, the true or higher Self of every man.

The empirical studies of psychotherapists have discovered, however, that beneath the conscious mind of man there is not only a vast depth of unconscious mentation, there is a common heritage of sub-rational and unconscious "mind" which is known to them as the collective unconscious. It is of unknowable extent and may reach to the limits of the within of creation. This within is static in that it is, yet dynamic in that it is becoming. The whole of creation is moving towards its fulfilment, and consciousness is collectivising in man as the Spirit inherent in things and behind all things becomes manifest. The conscious mind of man, both individual and collective is encompassing ever more and more, and moving towards an Omega-Point, an "end product" which St Paul, in a passage already quoted, sees as everything in heaven and on earth "brought together under Christ".

But there is more to the present within; it is claimed, and it is the experience of many men and women that the within is the present abode of discarnate men and women who are themselves active "for good" as it is represented to us.

Plato and the first verse of Genesis are agreed that God created "heaven" and "earth". The Upanishads, in part, tend towards that understanding, but man could only speculate until Revelation confirmed some speculations and corrected others. Plato spoke of the "world of Forms", of Ideas, of perfect archetypes, of which this world was but an imperfect replica, and Hebrew myth and apocalyptic could speak of the "Sons of God" attending upon Yahweh—meaning the holy angels (*Job 1:6*)—and the "Ancient of Days" and the "Son of Man" (*Dan 7*), while the prophets, in attempts to describe mystical experience could tell confusedly of the "Chariot of Yahweh" (*Ezek 1*) and the vision of God and his angels (*Isaiah 6*); but a clear statement of the reality of the heavenly state as something wholly "other" yet related came only with the New Testament, and to this I shall return at a later stage.

# 7

# Under the Earth

This study must be academic, but it is very important to remember that the "live" study of the underworld (for want of a better term) is anything but academic, for it is a matter of very widespread human experience in any society and in any generation that highly sensitive psychics are from time to time made aware of the objective presence of another human being who is, nevertheless, not "present" in the same way that they are. There is, too, an occasional awareness of a kind of telepathic communication which is at least possible. This is not the same thing altogether as the activity of trance mediums. The psychic sense works in a variety of ways and at several "levels", and there are a number of psychic "gifts". There is a kind of "freemasonry" of those who are psychically sensitive and who have an inherited and instinctive awareness of at any rate some levels of the within of things, and to whom encounter with the underworld comes as no great surprise.

Edward Conze, making reference to *The Tibetan Book of the Dead*, claims that it "represents Stone Age knowledge of life after death, and many other traditions, preserved in Egyptian, Persian and Christian writings, corroborate its revelations. It will seem pure nonsense to most of those who have undergone modern compulsory education. Professor Jung, however, prized it sufficiently to say that 'from the year of its appearance onwards the *Bardo* has been my constant companion'."[1]

It must be recognised that to a great number of Western Europeans, the whole subject of psychism is opaque and improbable. To any such among my readers I must apologise and ask of them that they allow

[1] Edward Conze, *Buddhist Scriptures*, p. 222.

the possibility that a dimension of perception exists of which they are unaware. Certainly in very primitive societies the veil between this world and the underworld is thin indeed, and it was a common custom in many magico-religious systems to offer human sacrifice (originally with willing victims, latterly with unwilling ones) with, as part at least of the intention, the securing thereby of a "contact" on the "other side", able theoretically to move freely in both time and space without let or hindrance. There have always been dark rituals with the intention of "binding" a soul to a place, and in obedience to a given magician. The construction of elemental beings on the inner planes (similar to poltergeists) is a more modern version of the same thing.

For the most part, the traditions of this "frontier" are communicated to the world at large through the medium of the novel, and Dennis Wheatley and Charles Williams are the best-known exponents of this form. Wheatley writes from an occult standpoint (with some licence, but less than might be supposed), and Williams, who was a profound scholar and lay theologian, writes as a deeply committed Christian. Of the latter's books, perhaps *Descent into Hell* and *All Hallows Eve* (his last) are the most revealing in the matters with which we are concerned. But despite Conze's reference to "Christian" writings, this is a subject which Christians hardly ever write about as Christians. Theologians tend to avoid the subject for the simple reason that, for the Christian as a Christian it has practically no interest whatever. The whole Christian eschatological hope is wholly differently orientated, and speculation about the underworld, and the deliberate cultivation of psychic sensitivity are sources of potential danger in that they have a fascination and can seduce a Christian away from that thing which alone matters to him, of which, more later.

The *Tibetan Book of the Dead* contains an instruction which a Lama reads to a dying person, telling him of the processes that must be undergone upon leaving this world. He is to remain "watchful and alert" and to be sure to be as aware as possible of the moment of his entry into the "intermediate state."

In all probability, it will have been taken for granted that the "Aperture of Brahma" will have been consciously opened, for it is through this aperture that the consciousness leaves the body for rebirth in the pure land. A detailed account of this process is given in *The Secrets of Chinese Meditation* by Lu K'uan Yü (pp. 193–201). But upon the moment of departure; "First of all there will appear to you, swifter than lightning, the luminous splendour of the colourless light of Emptiness, and that will surround you on all sides. Terrified, you will want to flee from the radiance, and you may well lose consciousness. Try to submerge yourself in that light, giving up all belief in a separate self, all attachment to your illusory ego. Recognize that the boundless Light of this true Reality is your own true self, and you shall be saved!

"If you miss salvation at that moment, you will be forced to have a number of further dreams, both pleasant and unpleasant. Even they offer you a chance to gain understanding, as long as you remain vigilant and alert. A few days after death there suddenly emerges a subtle illusory dream-body, also known as the 'mental body'. It is impregnated with the after-effects of your past desires, endowed with all sense-faculties, and has the power of unimpeded motion. . . . Even after the physical sense-organs are dissolved, sights, sounds, smells, tastes, and touches will be perceived, and ideas will be formed. These are the result of the energy still residing in the six kinds of consciousness, the after-effects of what you did with your body and mind in the past. But you must know that all you perceive is a mere vision, a mere illusion, and does not reflect any really existing objects. Have no fear, and form no attachment! View it all evenmindedly, without like or dislike!"[1]

It is worthwhile to quote this book at some length for, in part at least, it is true to the instinctive, unexpressed awarenesses of that universal "freemasonry" that I have mentioned. It must be remembered that this is a speculative work, however "scriptural" it may be in the Buddhist tradition. It must be remembered too that it presupposes the Buddhist doctrine of reincarnation, and therefore it is hard to say where insight ends and dogma begins (if true insight there be). Indeed the "salvation" referred to in many places in the text is salvation out of the cycle of incarnation and reincarnation. It is seen—with great profundity—as the identification of man with his True Self (his Atman),

[1] Conze, *op. cit.*, pp. 227–8.

but Buddhism tends to extend over unimaginable tracts of time, and many, many incarnations, the attainment of Buddhahood which passes into Nirvana, the state of final blessedness. Conze explains that, to Buddhists, "the 'gods' are in a way really 'angels', and their 'heavens' might also be called 'paradises'. Buddhist theology knows of about thirty kinds of gods, but the higher grades have a constitution so refined and a mode of life so unfamiliar that we could not easily form a concrete idea of their mode of existence. Detailed information is confined to the lowest heavens. . . . The 'hells' do not imply eternal damnation, and correspond perhaps more to the 'purgatory' of the Catholics."[1] The heavens and hells, Conze tells us, are the states in which people are rewarded and punished for their deeds, and "intermediary states" in which they pass the interval between death and rebirth. There are also the "Pure Lands" of the cosmic Buddhas. But to return to *The Book of the Dead.*

"Three and a half days after your death, Buddhas and Bodhisattvas will for seven days appear to you in their benign and peaceful aspect. Their light will shine upon you, but it will be so radiant that you will scarcely be able to look at it. Wonderful and delightful though they are, the Buddhas may nevertheless frighten you. Do not give in to your fright! Do not run away! Serenely contemplate the spectacle before you! Overcome your fear, and feel no desire! Realise that these are the rays of the grace of the Buddhas, who come to receive you into their Buddha-realms. Pray to them with intense faith and humility, and, in a halo of rainbow light, you will merge into the heart of the divine Father–Mother, and take up your abode in one of the realms of the Buddhas. Thereby you may still at this moment win your salvation.

"But if you miss it, you will next, for another seven days, be confronted with the angry deities, and the Guardians of the Faith, surrounded by their followers in a tumultuous array. . . . Do not give in to your fright, resist your mental confusion! All this is unreal, and what you see are the contents of your own mind in conflict with itself. . . . What you see here is but the reflection of the contents of your own mind in the mirror of the Void. If at this point you should manage to

[1] Conze, *op. cit.*, p. 221.

understand that, the shock of this insight will stun you, your subtle body will disperse into a rainbow, and you will find yourself in paradise among the angels. But if you fail to grasp the meaning of what you were taught, if you still continue to feel a desire to exist as an individual, then you are now doomed to again re-enter the wheel of becoming."[1]

This book is a classic; it contains much that is bizarre, and at best it must be regarded as speculation. But its insights into human psychology are profound, and any student of the subject will recognize the attractions that it had for Professor Jung.

Christian theology chooses to keep silence upon these matters, except for equally speculative attempts at rationalisation which have produced the doctrines (much disputed) of Purgatory and Limbo. We must needs turn to other sources, therefore, for a Christian is not, typically, an interested party as far as the contents and activities of the underworld are concerned. The Qabalistic mainstream of Western Occultism (to whom reference has already been made), maintains a doctrine of man which is by no means irreconcilable with that of Buddhism. "Briefly, the human being can be divided for purposes of analysis into three vehicles: the part of him which is eternal, the part of him that lasts as long as an evolution, and the part of him that lasts only a human lifetime in Earth. The first we will call the Spirit, the second the Individuality, and the third the Personality. The Spirit, when it enters the manifest Universe, has its own spiritual vehicle which projects into denser manifestation an evolving unit which we call the Individuality. This in turn projects into even denser manifestation a series of Personalities with which it gains experience of dense, worldly life. . . . In function, the Spirit is, by its very nature, perfect; but on account of what is generally called Original Sin or, more occultly, the Fall, or Prime Deviation, the Individuality is to some extent aberrated. That is to say, it is not a true reflection of the Spirit and thus though the author of apparently the highest motives, these motives may be wrong. As the Personality is a projection of the imperfect Individuality then it follows that the Personality is also

[1] Conze, *op. cit.*, pp. 228–9.

aberrated and this should be obvious from common sense observation of the state of the world we live in. . . . It is a great struggle for man to link up his Personality consciously with his Individuality, yet this is the first requisite of occult knowledge and power and should have been a natural phenomenon. The same applies with the conformity of the Individuality with the Will of the Spirit which marks the difference between White and Black Magic."[1]

The idea of reincarnation is common to most pre-Christian religious systems. From the occult doctrine we gather that man undergoes a number of "personalities" before he is able to graduate to permanent occupation of the Inner Planes. Another occult writer of considerable standing, Dion Fortune, in an intense and profound work which ranks almost as "scripture" for certain occultists, treats of the death of the Personality in terms not too dissimilar from the Tibetan work:

"The Personality, when withdrawn by death from the body, yet continues to live and function as a Personality, and the man is in no wise changed and still 'answers to the name he bore in the flesh'. In the Lower Hells he burns with desire until the possibilities of desire are burnt out. Desire then remains only as an abstract idea and is part of the Individuality. He then dies to the lower desires but continues to live in the higher desires.

"These in their turn he learns to be finite and mortal; he finds them to constitute barriers between himself and his Father whose face he would behold, and he desires to escape from them. He would no longer love with the personal love which loves a person, but with the higher manifestation of love which itself is Love and loves no person or thing but is a state of consciousness in which all is embraced. He then seeks freedom from the lesser love, and it is this desire for release from that which though good is finite in order to realize the good that is infinite which causes the Fifth Death, and he is born into consciousness of the Individuality, and lives upon the plane of the Individuality, perceiving the 'face of his Father Which is in Heaven'.

"But with the waking of desire come again the dreams, and with the dreams comes the recall into matter. The Spirit, beholding the face of

[1] Gareth Knight, *A Practical Guide to Qabalistic Symbolism*, vol 11, pp. iv–v.

its Father until consciousness is weary with Its brightness, closes its eyes and sleeps; and sleeping, it dreams of its unfulfilled desires and so it is born again, for upon the plane of desire a state of consciousness is a place, and as we desire, so are we reborn."[1]

*The Tibetan Book of the Dead*, less abstract and intense, nevertheless conveys much the same message. Yama, King of the Dead, holds up the "shining mirror of Karma". The soul passes judgement upon itself. Dion Fortune maintains "each man makes his own Karma". The glossary at the end of Conze's collection of Buddhist Scriptures defines Karma as "A volitional action which is either wholesome or unwholesome; and in consequence either rewarded or punished." Lu K'uan Yu, in his glossary defines it similarly as, "Moral action causing future retribution, and either good or evil transmigration." The freely willed actions of man contain their own built-in judgement and there is no escape from the consequences. Pre-Christian religion, Cosmos-bound, depends upon "the righteousness of the Law", be that religion Hebrew or Hindu. The one lives by the Law of Moses, the other the Law of Karma, inherent in creation. "The sting of death is sin, and sin gets its power from the Law." (*1 Cor 15:56*.)

The Tibetan book details the subjective terrors of retribution but reminds its reader that they "are just an illusion which you create from the forces within you. Know that apart from these karmic forces there is no Judge of the Dead, no gods, and no demons. Knowing that, you will be free."[2] But after the self-judgement; "at this juncture you will realise that you are dead. You will think, 'I am dead! What shall I do?' and you will feel as miserable as a fish out of water on red-hot embers. . . . at about that time the fierce wind of karma, terrific and hard to bear, will drive you onwards, from behind, in dreadful gusts. And after a while the thought will occur to you, 'O what would I not give to possess a body!' . . . Then there will shine upon you the lights of the six places of rebirth. The light of the place in which you will be reborn will shine most prominently, but it is your own karmic disposition which decides about your choice. . . . Your desire for rebirth becomes more and more urgent. . . . Everywhere around you, you will see

---

[1] Dion Fortune, *The Cosmic Doctrine*, pp. 121–2.
[2] Conze, *op cit.*, p. 230.

animals and humans in the act of sexual intercourse . . . do not go near the couples you see, do not try to interpose yourself between them, do not try to take the place of one of them! The feeling which you would then experience would make you faint away, just at the moment when egg and 'sperm are about to unite. And afterwards you will find that you have been conceived as a human being or as an animal."[1]

According to Buddhist understanding, the Buddha first began to prepare himself for Buddhahood after meeting Dipankara, his twenty-fourth predecessor, many "aeons" before his own final incarnation in the sixth century B.C. Buddhists assume that there are two kinds of time; historical—measured in years, and cosmic—measured in "aeons". The length of an "aeon" has been described, in the *Mahavastu*, as "in any case more than ten (years) followed by twenty-seven noughts!" It would not be too much of an exaggeration to describe the whole idea of rebirth, or reincarnation, as immediately alienating to the Christian; he is tempted to sweep it aside with impatience. The reasons are twofold; subjectively it is distasteful, and objectively it seems to deny both the doctrine of the Resurrection of the body and the finality of the redemption of man in Christ. But the subject demands a closer treatment than Christians are normally disposed to give it, and, although in the strictest sense reincarnation is of no consequence to the Christian and forms no part of the Gospel as he is bound to hold and proclaim it, it will be worth our while to return to the subject in a later chapter if only to "exorcise" the fears which may attend upon it.

It will be worth our while to close this chapter with Dion Fortune's description of Illumination, or as she calls it, the "Seventh Death". For this represents the kind of earthly perfection which is the best earthbound man can attain according to the tenets of pre-Christian religion. As in the first passage of hers quoted, she uses Christian terms without, however, meaning quite the same things by them as an orthodox Christian.

"In the Seventh Death consciousness is withdrawn from the Personality and made one with the Individuality and then a man beholds

---

[1] Conze, *op cit.*, pp. 230–232.

the face of his Father Which is in Heaven, even when he himself sojourns upon Earth. Thus it is that the illuminated Initiate is not as other men. Complete Initiation is a living death.

"Those who desire the things of the senses and the pride of life use the words 'living death' to denote the most terrible fate that can befall man; but those who have knowledge know that the 'living death' means the freedom of the spirit brought through to the plane of matter. It means the consciousness of the 'Abiding Presence' in the midst of the consciousness of the senses. It means awareness of Heaven while dwelling upon Earth. Therefore the Initiate goes to the living death which is freedom whilst still in the body, for death annuls the Law of Limitation, frees the potentialities of the spirit, gives sight to the blind and power to the impotent. That for which we longed vainly in life we realize in death, for death is life and life is death.

"To the wider consciousness the womb is a grave and the grave is a womb. The evolving soul, entering upon life, bids farewell to his friends who mourn him, and taking his courage in both hands and facing the great ordeal and submitting to suffering, enters upon life. His first action in life is to draw breath. His second action with that breath is to set up a cry of distress, because he has entered upon the task of life with grief; and his aim in life is to make life bearable. But when he enters the grave he passes through a gateway into the wider life of consciousness; and when the Initiate would pass to the wider life of consciousness, he passes to it through a gateway which symbolizes death; and by his death to the things of desire he obtains freedom, and as one dead he walks among men. In the death in life, which is the freedom of the spirit in the bonds of flesh, he transcends the Law of Limitation; being dead, he is free; being dead he moves with power among those buried in the flesh; and they, seeing the Light shining brightly through him, know that he is dead, for the Light cannot shine through the veil of flesh. While consciousness is incarnate in the body the Light cannot shine through that consciousness; but when consciousness is discarnate the Light shines through it. If the discarnate consciousness is still manipulating its body, then that Light shines through into the world of matter and illuminates men. But remember this, and meditate upon it—the illuminated Initiate is a dead man who manipulates his body that he may thereby serve those who cannot otherwise be approached."[1]

The eschatological hope of man, in the systems considered, may be described in one of two ways: If he is an Old Testament Hebrew, he hopes that God will intervene and turn the merry go round of earthly life into earthly bliss and, at some undefined end, stop it and resurrect the dead from out of Sheol that they may once more enjoy it. If he is a Hindu, a Buddhist or an Occultist, he seeks to graduate to that degree of initiation or perfection that will allow him to jump off the merry go round while it is still moving. This first section began with the proclamation of Genesis that "in the beginning God created the heavens and the earth". It is clear beyond doubt that we are still stuck fast in the good mud of "the earth".

[1] Fortune, *op. cit.*, pp. 122–3.

*Part Two*

A Necessary Digression

# 8

# All is not well

The section which now follows is an unavoidable digression. It would be sensible, having spent some chapters thinking specifically of the "earth" and its within, to proceed with a discussion of "the heavens" and of the relationship that might be perceived as existing between them. But this cannot be. For something has gone wrong with "the earth", and first there must be some consideration of what can possibly be meant by the concepts of "original sin" and "the fall".

The idea has already been encountered in a quotation from occult writing upon the threefold nature of man. The "prime deviation" was claimed as having been instrumental in aberrating both individuality and personality according to that doctrine. Doctrines vary from tradition to tradition, but the fact of human moral aberration is of universal experience, and the various theologies (which are, of course, collections of working hypotheses) have sought to deal with this inconvenient fact according to their various understandings of the nature of God, the Nature of creation, and the relationship between them.

The perversity and disharmony of mankind, a matter of universal experience and observation, exercised the Buddha, Confucius and Lao-Tse, whose teachings abounded with the most admirable and indeed inspired good sense, and the most unexceptionable and exalted moral philosophy. "If only men will do this, and live thus," they all said (in various ways), "all will be well". And men in their countless millions through the ages have agreed wholeheartedly and have devoted themselves to lives of veneration of the Sages' wisdom, while at the same time entirely failing to do what the Sages suggest. In terms of various religious and metaphysical traditions, this simple but glaring failure must be accounted for and a working hypothesis arrived at which, as far as may be, fits the bill. In Christian terms the hypotheses in question are known as the doctrines of original sin and of the fall.

As man has advanced in his understanding of himself and his milieu, two sharply conflicting principles have presented themselves and have vied with each other for the exercise both of his judgement and his free will. These principles are those commonly called "good" and "evil", but such a simple bestowal of titles belies the complexity and the subtlety of the problems that these phenomena bring. Man's efforts to explain and to reconcile the principles, and to construct a working hypothesis, have produced a wide variety of doctrines. But the general pre-Christian tendency, variously expressed, has been towards a rejection of the phenomenal world as something unsatisfactory by its very nature; a situation to be escaped from. The world (in the Platonic view) is the imperfect replica of the perfect Idea, and thus the realm of "ideas" is the desired refuge. In the main, pre-Christian religion rejects the world as a veil of tears and seeks permanent release from its miseries in a purely "spiritual" and discarnate existence. The idea of the "immortality of the soul" belongs to this general climate of opinion. Contrary to popular belief, it is not at all a Christian doctrine.

Pre-Christian religion is, as we have seen already, very essentially, and entirely properly, earthbound. It must, of necessity, look to the within, to the inner planes for its future hope, and does so either confidently (as in Buddhism) or resignedly (as in Old Testament Judaism). The occult plays a great part in all pre-Christian religion, especially at popular level. Psychism can claim a degree at least of experiential knowledge of the hereafter. To primitive man, the question of life after death is no question at all, for a primitive, psychically orientated society has experience enough and to spare of the reality of the "other side". The within of the phenomenal world, the inner planes, represents, a very considerable part of that field of activity which pre-Christian religion would regard as "Spirituality" and "Mysticism". Here is the great and essential divide between the Spirituality of the pre-Christian and Christian religions! The Christian would very properly regard all this as psychism and not at all as mysticism. Spirituality and mysticism proper are concerned with wholly "other" things, to which we shall return on a later page. The classics of Christian mysticism have nothing to say about a shadowy continuence in a shadowy within, they are concerned with other matters altogether, and wholly "other" dimensions, and the only references made to psychic matters (by, for example, St John of the Cross) are in the nature of warnings lest they be regarded as important or truly spiritual in nature!

Man has developed a tendency to establish a kind of dichotomy between material and spiritual; between sacred and secular. This very much pre-Christian (indeed non-Christian) idea has had considerable currency within the Church, especially in the Reformed traditions. So powerful was its influence generally that it required a high degree of moral daring and theological integrity for Teilhard de Chardin, in the early nineteen-twenties, to dedicate *Le Milieu Divin*, "for those who love the world". And this in spite of the central fact of the Christian belief that "God loved the world so much that he gave his only Son." (*Jn 3:18.*)

The Christian Revelation appears, at first sight, to have made the problem of evil even more acute than it was before. Holy Scripture tells us that, in the beginning, God created, and all that was created was "good". God (if God there be) must be wholly omnipotent and omnipresent; wholly Transcendent and wholly Immanent. God, as man seeks to comprehend him, must be Holiness, Love, Justice. How can anything which is objectively "evil", anything objectively "not good", exist within a created order in which the Transcendent Creator is also Immanent? And yet the fact of evil—a kind of objective unreality—is manifest, and brought into the sharpest relief of all by that very Revelation which would seem to preclude its possibility!

Pierre Teilhard de Chardin, in a collection of papers and essays published posthumously, proclaims the Christ to be universal and cosmic in the best Pauline tradition, and claims: "*If Christ is to be truly universal*, the Redemption, and hence the Fall, must extend to the whole universe. Original sin accordingly takes on a *cosmic nature* that tradition has always accorded to it, but which, in view of the new dimensions we recognise in our universe, obliges us radically to restate the historical representation of that sin and the too purely juridical way in which we commonly describe its being passed on."[1]

[1] Teilhard de Chardin, *Science and Christ*, p. 16.

Teilhard has little to say on this subject, but the reason for this is probably more closely connected with obedience to his religious superiors than theological hesitancy on his part. The rough draft of a paper dealing with these matters fell into the hands of the censors in Rome in the early nineteen-twenties, and the resulting troubles for its author probably inhibited any further speculation. It is significant that there is an absence of any treatment of these important matters in his prolific writings after 1924. But in the collection of essays to which we have referred, he advances a tentative solution which it is worth quoting at some length.

"God did not will individually (nor could he have constructed as though they were separate bits), the sun, the earth, plants, or Man. *He willed his Christ*; (my italics)—and in order to have his Christ, he had to create the spiritual world, and man in particular, upon which Christ might germinate;—and to have man, he had to launch the vast process of organic life (which, accordingly, is not superfluity, but an essential organ of the world);—and the birth of that organic life called for the entire cosmic turbulence.

"At the beginning of the perceptible world what existed was the Multiple; and that Multiple was already rising up, like one indissociable whole, towards spirit under the magnetic influence of the universal Christ who was being engendered in it. This ascent was slow and painful; for from that moment the Multiple was, through something in itself, evil.

"Whence did the universe acquire its original stain? Why are we obliged in some way to identify evil and matter, evil and determinisms, evil and plurality? Is it only because, in relation to our souls, the lower zones of the universe and of union are a country that has been left behind—that is therefore forbidden—to fall back into which is to be corrupted? Or is it not, rather, as the Bible would seem categorically to assert, because the original Multiple was born from the dissociation of an already unified being (the First Adam), with the result that, in this present period of history, the world is not rising up towards Christ (the Second Adam) but *resuming its ascent*. [My italics.]

"Whichever hypothesis is accepted, that Evil pluralised the world as a consequence of a culpable act—or that the world (because it is plural, evolutionary) produced Evil, at the very first instant, as an object produces its shadow—in either case creative union has the particular characteristic of being a redemptive union. God seems to have been unable to create without engaging in a struggle against evil at the same time as against the Multiple."[1]

Teilhard says practically nothing else about original sin and the fall. On the last page of *The Phenomenon of Man*, having tried hard to reconcile "evils" of disorder and failure, of decomposition and of growth— "evils" in the sense of being sources of suffering, tears and blood—he asks, "But is that really all? Is there nothing else to see? In other words, is it really sure that, for an eye trained and sensitised by light other than that of pure science, the quantity and malice of evil *hic et nunc*, spread through the world, does not betray a certain *excess*, inexplicable to our reason, if *to the normal effect of evolution* is not added the *extraordinary effect* of some catastrophe or primordial deviation? On this question, in all loyalty, I do not feel I am in a position to take a stand."[2]

Christian theology has argued at the greatest length over the uncomfortable fact of sin and the inbuilt aberration of the human will. John Hick, in his *Evil and the God of Love*, gives a masterly and comprehensive summary of the hypotheses of Christian theologians through the ages, and it will not be the task of this book to seek to do the same in what is, after all, an extended parenthesis. But I shall seek to cover some at least of the ground that theologians prefer to avoid, and to discover something of the doctrines of the pre-Christian religious traditions that have already been considered in the first section.

[1] Teilhard de Chardin, *Science and Christ*, pp. 79–80.
[2] Teilhard de Chardin, *The Phenomenon of Man*.

# 9

# It is all His fault!

Man's temptation to blame God for the existence of evil is considerable. Adam, in the myth of the Garden of Eden, blames God by implication with his answer, "the woman you gave me . . . she gave me . . .
and I ate." A very typically human response, and one with which all men
are at some time or another identified. Eve implies a complaint against
the management at having to contend with an existing corrupting influence when she answers, "the serpent tricked me, and I ate." The implication is (and man is quick to take it up) that it was unsatisfactory of
God to put man in a position in which he was almost certain to fall
from grace. In the words of the Curé d'Ars (in another context
altogether), "it is no use throwing straw on a fire and telling it not to
burn!"

The Garden of Eden situation speaks to man's experience of things.
Evil, which ought to be impossible, appears to exist as an objective
fact, independent of man. This fact of human experience is never
satisfactorily resolved by the monist theologies of Hinduism and Buddhism. The law of Karma covers all aspects of human behaviour, and
things work themselves out over aeons of time. There are orders of
spirits, and at popular level, spiritism in all forms is rife. But the scriptures tend to transcend all this and have little to say about it. The "hells"
are private and subjective. They are also temporary.

The Qabalistic mainstream of the occult tradition of the West, which
is the only monistic religious system in the Western Hemisphere,
maintains a doctrine of original sin and the fall which relates to the
essentially emanationist theology of creation which is shared, generally
speaking, with Hinduism and Buddhism. Briefly, the Qabalistic
belief is that God emanates that which we should describe as creation,
the cosmos, through ten successive stages of manifestation, the final

stage being the phenomenal world. Between the first three, Supernal, stages and the remaining seven, there is the Abyss, which is caused by the fall, or, in occult terminology, the Prime Deviation. W. G. Grey, in his excellent book *The Ladder of Lights*, outlines the Qabalistic occultists' concept of Divine Error. It will be found to echo, in some respects, Teilhard de Chardin's speculations recorded in the previous chapter, and we shall quote it at some length.

"The old Qabalists gave the Abyss the name of Masak Mavdil, meaning a place for rejected failures, and it was presided over by a sort of Angel or genius whose name was Mesukiel, or Ridya, meaning 'The Veiler of God'. There was a teaching to the effect that at least three previous Creations had been made by God prior to ours, and being unsatisfied with them, the Great One swept them away into the Abyss which was created as a sort of Divine dust-bin. This is not only very interesting, but it explains why so little has been said of the Abyss in Qabalistic writings. The inference is that the Divine One is not only capable of producing unsatisfactory work, but has even appointed a special angel to conceal the fact."[1]

The old Qabalists that Grey refers to would be, in the main, the Jewish Qabalists from whom the Gentile occultism took over the Qabalah. There is a continuing stream of Qabalism in Judaism to this day, but it is very different from Gentile occultism, for it is maintained in Jewish orthodoxy by the "oral Torah" (discussed in the first chapter) of which it is a part. But Grey continues with his doctrine of "Divine Error" and maintains that "a refusal to see mistakes or inaccuracies in the part of God has blinded man to many Inner Truths. Orthodox religions have quite failed to grasp the importance or significance of this secret teaching. Apart from explaining many evident anomalies, it points quite clearly to the tremendous role of Mankind in the Divine Plan. We may be one of God's biggest mistakes, but we are a self-correcting one in the long run, for it must never be forgotten that no matter what goes wrong, the Perpetual Divine Intention is no less than Absolute Perfection, and that all that fails to reach that point will be eventually discarded in the Abyss. Nothing essentially wrong in itself

[1] W. G. Grey, *The Ladder of Lights*, p. 150.

will survive the crossing of that Chasm. According to legend, the Abyss acts as a sort of filter trap. . . . All the horrors, loathsomeness, abominations, and evils that would be unthinkable in association with a God fundamentally connected to pure Goodness are swallowed by the Abyss, where they exist in a state of completely insane chaos pending some ultimate disposal."[1]

The Abyss, thus described, performs much the same function as "Gehenna", the Jerusalem Corporation Rubbish Dump (in our Lord's image), rendered in the New Testament by the English word "hell". There is, however, no suggestion of Divine Error by the Son of God. Nevertheless, the dilemma remains unresolved in man's mind.

Grey outlines the occult doctrines both of the fall and of redemption. He is concerned with what Qabalists call "Daath", which for our present purposes we may understand as a kind of blank space in the scheme of things, which is, as it were, suspended over the Abyss as a mystical "bridge" between the Supernals and the rest of manifesting creation which culminates in the phenomenal world. "The word 'Daath' by itself signifies Knowledge of the type gained by experience and effort. It can also mean self-knowledge in the sense of auto-awareness. Daath is the objective referred to by the well-known dictum: 'Man Know Thy Self'. It is an acquired knowledge rather than an inherent faculty."[2] Grey enlarges upon his theme, and refers back to the beginning of things, when God first began to emanate what is known to us as creation. "At this stage, however, there was no objective creation to be conscious of. *God was conceived but not born.* [My italics.] Knowledge sought Experience, which could scarcely be obtained without material. So Daath 'fell', or was born into matter where it became (the phenomenal world), leaving a gap in its original place which is now the Abyss."[3] The suggestion is that God himself had to "fall" in order to "know". There is something at least of an echo here of Teilhard's understanding that, having "willed his Christ", God was inevitably involved in the whole business of creation, including all its contradictions, and in addition the whole business of redemption as a consequence of those contradictions. Grey continues: "Thus commenced the whole scheme of

[1] W. G. Grey, *The Ladder of Lights*, p. 151.    [2] *Ibid.*, p. 157.    [3] *Ibid.*, p. 157.

Redemption, which means to us that Man must return to God through the Way of Knowledge and ultimately (the phenomenal world) will be restored to its proper place . . . as Completed Consciousness. The original 'Fall' was not that of Man, but of God Who sought Knowledge through the Experience of Man. This was the 'expulsion from Paradise'. Man was projected from subjective existence in the Divine Consciousness into a state of separated objectivity, becoming a being with limited self-determination. We can imagine this almost as if a solitary person created a subjective personality in (himself) which grew into such a positive existence that it materialised into independent life from its creator.

"Such is our so-called 'free-will'. From being a controlled thought in the Divine Mind, Man was externalised as a reflective image of the Divinity which had a similitude of self-expression in its own sphere. This meant the Man-part of Expressed Divinity must needs be given the ability to determine itself apart from the God-part. Otherwise there could be no mutual interchange of consciousness through Creation. Man must be able to disagree with or disobey the Divine Mind if he felt like it, for unless this were possible, he could not act as a reactive stimulator of the Consciousness which created him.

"So we 'fell from Paradise' as Lucifer 'fell from Heaven'. The two 'Falls' are really one experience undergone by differing types of being. Man fell by the tree of Knowledge (Daath) and rises by the Tree of life. Lucifer fell by refusing to recognise Man, and can only rise as Mankind releases him. Both Man and Lucifer hold each other captive on different levels, and Daath marks the point of our fall and our Redemption. God may redeem man, but Man redeems Lucifer. Much may be learned from this Mystery . . . Daath . . . is essentially (the phenomenal world) before and after perfection through experience. We can think of it as being . . . 'in the making' as it were, by the combined efforts of Divinity and Humanity. Together, God and Man share the common Sphere of Knowledge."[1]

This passage, quoted at some length, is as lucid a statement as may be found of a doctrine of the fall and of redemption which belongs to a

[1] *Ibid.*, pp. 157–8.

theological system, which in some sense at any rate, identifies the Creator with his Creation in however developed and sophisticated a way. The passage abounds with profound and sometimes disturbing insights. The Qabalist's "Tree of Life", the diagrammatic representation of the process of emanation, is a very plausible "road map" of the within of the created order, and certainly so for occult purposes. As a working hypothesis it serves the occultist well in his quest to "become God" (or perhaps to return to Divinity, or realise the Divinity inherent in his being) by a deliberate plunge into the within of the created order. By the selfsame token, the Hindu and the Buddhist seek to identify their Atman with the Brahman by techniques which are often far from dissimilar. Occultism, Hinduism and Buddhism have this much in common, that they are, each of them, a Dharma, and seek identical ends in similar ways because their end-in-view is the totality of the cosmos: "The earth", rather than "the heavens".

The Qabalistic doctrine that we have studied has one great advantage, and one that naturally attracts fallen man, in that it removes most of the guilt from original sin. The fall is, after all, God's doing, even if we may not actually say God's fault. Grey says, that of our own sins, "very many of our troubles on all levels are brought upon us by our retention of useless and deteriorating material in our spiritual, mental and physical systems. Instead of eliminating it and obtaining fresh supplies of energy, we accumulate it inside us where it simply goes bad and spreads poisons of corruption until they kill us. Diseases of the body usually start in the soul and mind where festering hates and resentments together with other impurities are gathered in dangerous combinations. We should learn how to evacuate them completely out of us into the Abyss, so we become entirely free from their contamination and are able to take in fresh clean energies to replace them. This is the true 'Forgiveness of Sins'; that we clear ourselves utterly . . ."[1]

There can be no real understanding of God's forgiveness in a monistic system. If God is capable of error, then he is neither in the position of being able to wholly condemn, nor wholly forgive. If man is not wholly responsible for his error, if free-will is less than free, then he needs no forgiveness from a God to whom he can complain of

[1] W. G. Grey, *The Ladder of Lights*, p. 156.

irresponsibility. Salvation is an automatic business, depending upon self-help and the knowledge of the proper techniques.

If monism is to be a really workable hypothesis, it must arrive at some such concept as reincarnation, and indeed all the monistic theologies do so arrive. The magician attains to the fullness of the Macrocosm through many incarnations. The Hindu's Atman is finally identified with Brahman after many incarnations and Buddhahood is only reached after many, many aeons. The doctrine of Karma covers all eventualities. It is not sufficient to regard Karma as a system of "blind, cosmic justice" for the concept is more subtle than this. A man, in incarnation, must play the hand he is given as best he can, and upon his play will depend the cards dealt to him in his next incarnation. There can be no sense of history in a monist's cosmos, no essential process in the sum of things. A wholly Immanent God is both inhibited and introverted, and his creation is essentially static.

# 10

# Obey! Or Else!

The prophet Mohammed, at the age of forty, received a series of revelations which served to convince him that his vocation was to be God's messenger, charged with the duty of confirming the Will of God as revealed through Old and New Testament prophets, but perverted (as he believed) by their later followers. This remarkable man, the son, born posthumously, of Abdullah bin Abdul-Muttalib of Mecca, compiled, at various times, a series of commentaries upon the Old Testament and such of the New Testament as was familiar to him which, together, form the *Koran*, the Holy Scriptures of Islam. It seems clear that Mohammed was influenced in early life, and probably to a considerable extent, by both Jews resident in Mecca, and also heretical Christian sects which were as abundant then as now. His evident misunderstanding (in Christian eyes) of many of the Christian traditions would indicate this, and the scandal of schism and sectarianism provoked his bitter condemnation. Mohammed conceived it to be his prophetic duty to call men back to the true faith delivered to Abraham, and this he interpreted as absolute submission and resignation to the will of God.

N. J. Dawood, in the introduction to his translation of the Koran into English, says "the Koran preaches the oneness of God and emphasises divine mercy and forgiveness. God is almighty and all-knowing, and though compassionate towards His creatures, He is stern in retribution. He enjoins justice and fair dealing, kindness to orphans and widows, and charity to the poor. The most important duties of the Muslim are faith in Allah and His apostle, prayer, alms-giving, fasting, and pilgrimage to the Sacred House at Mecca, built by Abraham for the worship of the One God."[1]

[1] N. J. Dawood, *The Koran* (tr), p. 10.

The Koran is first and foremost a commentary upon the Old
Testament and a correction to the New, and contains some original
matter. Islam, is in its own estimation, the natural successor and fulfilment of the religion of Israel. The tone of the two scriptures is
markedly different, however. Islam sees God as wholly transcendent,
wholly "other". The ends towards which man may look are either
Paradise or everlasting Hell-fire. Paradise is described in very anthropomorphic terms in the Koran. "Dark eyed houris" await the Faithful,
and the delights of the hereafter are described in orgiastic language.
But this is by no means an exclusively Muslim phenomenon, for the
*Paradise of Indra*, a tradition common to both Hinduism and Buddhism,
speaks of "celestial nymphs", and a classical poem, *Nanda the Fair*,
concerns Nanda, a relative of the Buddha, who was tempted to abandon
his monastic vocation in order to return to the arms of his wife. In
order to restore him to grace, he was granted a vision of Paradise:

"Nanda looked at Indra's grove, in all directions, with eyes wide
open and astonished. But the celestial nymphs exuberantly came round
him, and eyed each other in high spirits. When he saw that world to
be one long round of merry-making, and that no tiredness, sleepiness,
discontent, sorrow, and disease existed anywhere, the world of men
seemed no better to him than a cemetery, as being under the sway of
old age and death, and as always being in distress. Just as the sun,
when it rises, eclipses the light of a lamp lit when it was dark, so the
glory of the celestial nymphs nullifies the lustre of all merely human
women."[1]

In the Buddhist understanding, this jolly, Paradisal state of affairs is
but temporary, a reward for a well-spent incarnation before returning
to the world again. But in Islamic eyes it seems to be permanent, at
least until the Last Judgement and the Day of Resurrection, of which
much is said in the Koran, but after which, it is not clear what is to be.
In Paradise, however,

"They shall dwell with bashful virgins whom neither man nor
jinee will have touched before them." (*The Merciful.*)

In the chapter headed *The Believers*, the Koran records Allah as saying
to the Faithful: "You shall surely die hereafter, and be restored to

[1] E. Conze, *Buddhist Scriptures*, pp. 223-4.

life on the Day of Resurrection. We have created seven heavens above you; of Our creation We are never heedless."

However, metaphysics is not an Islamic concern by any means, and the reference to "seven heavens" may be paralleled in very many Gnostic writings and popular traditions of which St Paul makes mention in talking about his own prayer-life. (2 Cor 12:2.) Mysticism is, if anything, even less of a typically Islamic concern than metaphysics. Nevertheless it is remarkable what survives under this stark, puritan religious system. St Thomas Aquinas discovered Aristotle via the Arabs, and the Sufi mystics spoke in language very similar indeed to that of the great Spanish mystics of the sixteenth century.

But our present concern is with the fall and with the concept of original sin, and the Koran, in a commentary on the creation of myths, Genesis, makes plain the Islamic understanding of these phenomena. Allah, the Compassionate, the Merciful, says:

"We created man from dry clay, from black moulded loam, and before him Satan from smokeless fire. Your Lord said to the angels: 'I am creating man from dry clay, from black moulded loam. When I have fashioned him and breathed of my spirit into him, kneel down and prostrate yourselves before him.' All the angels prostrated themselves, except Satan. He refused to prostrate himself. 'Satan,' said Allah, 'why do you not prostrate yourself?' He replied: 'I will not bow down to a mortal created of dry clay, of black moulded loam.' 'Begone,' said Allah, 'you are accursed. My curse shall be on you till Judgement-Day.' 'Lord,' said Satan, 'reprieve me till the Day of Resurrection.' He answered: 'You are reprieved till the Appointed Day.' 'Lord,' said Satan, 'since you have led me astray, I will seduce mankind on earth: I will seduce them all, except those that faithfully serve you.' He replied: 'This is the right course for Me. You shall have no power over My servants, except the sinners who follow you. They are all destined for Hell.'" (Al-Hijr.)

Allah, the Compassionate, the Merciful, is also totally arbitrary, and there is no questioning of his arrangements. The Koran makes at least one other mention of this matter in the section called The Cow.

"We said to the angels: 'Prostrate yourselves before Adam,' they all prostrated themselves except Satan, who in his pride refused and became an unbeliever. To Adam We said: 'Dwell with your wife in Paradise and eat of its fruits to your hearts content wherever you will. But never approach this tree or you shall both become transgressors.' But Satan made them fall from Paradise and brought about their banishment."

The difference in tone between the first chapters of Genesis and *Al-Hijr* and *The Cow* is very marked. Absolute submission and resignation is indeed the only possible response of man to God as Mohammed conceives him.

Satan, in Islamic eyes, is a tester and tormenter of men on earth. Man is as solely responsible for his own reactions as he is understood to be in Hinduism or Buddhism. There is no clear doctrine of the aberration of the will by original sin. If man sins, then he will be punished:

"When Our judgement has been passed, Satan will say to (sinners): 'True was the promise which Allah made you. I too made you a promise, but did not keep it. Yet I had no power over you. I called you and you answered me. Do not now blame me, but blame yourselves. I cannot help you, nor can you help me. I never believed that I was Allah's equal.' " (*Abraham.*)

In the chapter called *The Imrans*, we are told that:

"It is Satan that prompts men to fear his followers. But have no fear of them. Fear Me, if you are true believers. Do not grieve for those that quickly renounce their faith. They will not harm Allah in the least. He seeks to give them no share in the hereafter. Their punishment shall be terrible indeed."

The Koran has a very great deal to say about Hell, and, in the Koran Hell is invariably the place of perpetual torment. But there is a change of emphasis from the New Testament Gehenna from which the Islamic concept probably owes its origin. It is very probably the case that our Lord intends us to understand Gehenna, "the perpetually burning rubbish-dump", to be eternal rather than the punishment it inflicts. We do not know if the outcome of Hell for a soul is total extinction or the horrifying possibility (mentioned somewhere by C. S. Lewis) of a conscious state of "having been a human soul". The idea that the torment is everlasting is supported by the Authorised Version's unhappy use of the word "hell" to translate both Gehenna and Hades/Sheol. Thus, in the parable of Dives and Lazarus, Dives, "in agony in these flames" (*Lk 16:19–31*) is in Hades—the underworld, the place of the dead—and not Gehenna, the end of the damned. Dives is undergoing purgation, not damnation. He is in Purgatory. It is not possible, in strict faithfulness to the Gospels, to proclaim with certainty that the punishment is everlasting although the fire may be.

In the Koran, however, both the place of torment and the torment itself are understood as being perpetual, and it is none other than Allah, the Compassionate, the Merciful who orders it. The Keepers of Hell are among the Faithful. In *The Ornaments of Gold*, one of them, Malek (a common Islamic name), in response to the pleas of the damned to be finally extinguished and removed from existence, answers: "Here you shall remain." And, in *The Pilgrimage*, it is said of the damned:

"Whenever, in their anguish, they try to escape from Hell, the angels will drag them back, saying: 'Taste the torment of Hell-fire'."

Again, in the chapter called *Women*:

"The angels will ask the men whom they carry off while steeped in sin: 'What were you doing?'"

The New Testament concept of the role of the angels at the Judgement is made most explicit in Matthew (*3:36–43*) where "the reapers are the angels" who will gather out of God's Kingdom "all things that provoke offences and all who do evil, and throw them into the blazing furnace." Typically, in the New Testament, the eschatological role of the angels is to "gather his *chosen* from the four winds, from the ends of the world to the ends of heaven" (*Mk 13:27*). The New Testament is always positive. Hell is the absence of Heaven; it is unreality, the absence of Reality. The tone of the Koran is very different.

The idea of divinely-ordered punishment, inflicted by good and faithful torturers, is by no means confined to Islam, however. In the *Middling Collection* of the *Pali Canon* of the Buddhist scriptures, Yama, king of the dead, is discovered wishing that he too could incarnate and thus aspire to Buddhahood.

"How much I wished that I could become a human being, at a time when a Tathagata arises in the world, an Arhat, a fully enlightened Buddha. Then I could pay homage to the Lord, and the Lord would teach me the Dharma, and I could thoroughly comprehend the Lord's Dharma!"[1]

Yama, king of the dead, longs to be a really good Buddhist. The punishments he inflicts are only temporary, between incarnations of those punished, and he is only terrible to the subjective vision of the condemned who see their own horror reflected in him. But in the Islamic tradition, the punishment is eternal, and the Keepers of Hell, faithful to Allah, inflict perpetual, intolerable torture.

The Islamic doctrine, such as it is, of original sin and the fall, is arbitrary and unsatisfying. A Christian might find it to be both derivative and distorted. But in this tradition, as in the occult tradition, is rooted a doctrine of an interrelated fall from grace both of angels and men.

It is easy to detect Christian influences behind both these non-Christian doctrines, but we must remember that they have both had to stand the test of human experience within the contexts of the religious systems of which they are expressions. As working hypotheses they will have had to be seen to "work". But the time has now come to turn our attention to the classical Biblical doctrines of the fall and of original sin before we resume the main burden of this work, and begin to think in terms of Heaven.

[1] E. Conze, *Buddhist Scriptures*, p. 226.

# Rock Bottom

In his renowned Bampton Lectures on original sin and the fall, N. P. Williams summarised the orthodox Christian doctrine—that working hypothesis based upon the Revelation of our Lord Jesus Christ—as follows:

"God is perfectly good and all his creation is created good. The origins of evil are to be sought in the voluntary rebellion of created wills, angelic and human. Man, at first, was weak, imperfect, ignorant and non-moral, but possessed self-consciousness and free-will as a starting-point for progress towards union with God. Man, as his moral ideas grew, disobeyed God, threw in his lot with the fallen angels (devils or demons) thereby, and diverged from his path. This act we call the Fall. Since the Fall, human nature has an inherent bias towards sin. This bias is due to the crippling of the will, which is no longer in control of the functions. The lower nature is only defectively controlled by the higher. This weakness is hereditary."

This concise summary represents the essential skeleton of Christian orthodox doctrine of original sin and the fall, but it is one that is constantly under debate. With each new insight into the psychological make-up of man, and the manner in which species evolve, theologians question the established doctrines and test them against the newest insights. In particular, in a generally agnostic and technologically minded age, the concept of angelic or demonic influence, is to say the least, unfashionable. Thus John Hick, in his *Evil and the God of Love*, to which reference has already been made, is content to say of angelic or demonic influence, "While we cannot, and have no wish to, exclude such possibilities, neither can we properly build any specific theological conclusions upon them."[1] On the face of things, and in consideration

[1] John Hick, *Evil and the God of Love*, pp. 203-4.

of Holy Scripture and our Lord's repeated references, this is a remarkable statement. But the insistence upon rationality alone is neither surprising nor culpable. Man is a reasoning creature and it is the task of the academic to reconcile faith with reason and not (if he can avoid it) to introduce "jokers" into the play. Angels, be they fallen or unfallen, belong to an order of being which is "other", and are not perceived (in so far as they are perceived at all) by the human intellect; an intellectual exercise cannot therefore be expected to attend to them other than in passing.

Nevertheless, a theology of original sin and the fall which is merely an exercise in human rationality will be arid, will fail to speak to the realities of human experience, and will be unfaithful to Revelation. Angels, fallen and otherwise, must, in the last resort, be taken seriously.

Intellectualism on its own can go so far and no further. It is right, however, that it should try to go as far as it can. Thus the publication of Darwin's *The Origin of Species* in 1859, and his *Descent of Man* in 1871 (not to mention the grotesque debate in the Royal Society in 1860 involving Bishop Wilberforce in controversy with the leading scientists of his day) prompted theology to incorporate the new concepts into its thinking. Thus an "evolutionary theory" of sin emerged which is best stated (and most briefly) in Tennyson's *In Memoriam*:

> "Move upward, working out the beast,
> And let the ape and tiger die."

The brave new world was in process of evolution. The passions appropriate in animals would hang on in men for a little longer, but evolution and the advances in education and science would dispose of them in due course. Failing this, our growing understanding of these passions may lead us to find them still, happily, appropriate in us. But in any event, in the words of J. Addington Symonds hymn:

> "Every life shall be a song,
> When all the earth is paradise."

The positive insights consequent upon the discovery of the ways in which creatures evolve and man's psychology functions are now

almost a commonplace, but the brave new "evolutionary theory" of
sin and the fall is dated, superficial and forgotten. Sin is a matter of the
will, and the realities involved in original sin and the fall lie deeper than
that brief, hopeful theory could penetrate. When all was said and done,
it was not true to Scripture, nor was it true to human experience.

It is easy to demolish, at least to one's own satisfaction, a theory of
original sin and the fall which, at heart, confines its vision to mere
biology, and which is the fruit of too quick and too shallow a reaction
to the challenge of the doctrine of the evolution of species. But there is
some method even in theological madness, for man is as adept at
constructing Absolutes in the field of morality as he is adept in constructing Absolutes in any other field. St Augustine's dictum; "Love
God, and do what you like", demands a degree of individual responsi-
bility that men shy away from instinctively. The thoughtful mind of
man knows itself incapable of living by such a "new morality" and is
quick to abdicate Love in favour of Law. It is a new Law that man is
always hoping to discover; he prefers bondage to an easier Law to the
total but terrible freedom of Love.

The underlying weakness of an evolutionary theory of original sin
and the fall one, that is, that will gradually "explain it away" is that it is
earthbound, and in the most superficial way. It has nothing to say
about the within, and yet it is manifestly the within that is deranged!
It follows that the origins of sin and the fall itself must be found to lie,
in some sense, in the within of things, and mere theorising about their
outward manifestations, individual or social, will do no more than
scratch the surface of the problem. We are back to Christian orthodoxy
before we know where we are. Islam and occultism support us (in
their various ways), and the Old Testament has not the slightest
hesitation in going straight to the heart of things in both of the myths
dealing with the origins of original sin.

"When mankind began to increase and to spread all over the earth
and daughters were born to them, the sons of the gods saw that the
daughters of men were beautiful; so they took for themselves such
women as they chose . . ." (*Gen 6:1:4.*)

This fragment is obscure and confused, but one understanding at least is that evil on earth originates from a source other than human, and it is this source which has corrupted man. The "sons of God" appear again as "the Court of Heaven" (*Job 1:6*), and Satan is found to be among them. I shall return to this fragment in a little while.

The more important myth is that of the Garden of Eden. A truly Teilhardian doctrine of the evolution of man as "the axis and leading shoot of evolution" is implicit in the very names of archetypal man and woman. In Gen 2:7, "man" (that is to say, "mankind") is Adam, a word originating from *Adamah*, meaning "the dust of the ground" from which he was formed. Mankind is differentiated into "man" (*Ish*) and "woman" (*Ishshah*), and the name of mankind's wife is Eve, which means "life". It is "conscious, living mud" we may say, that God makes into his own image and likeness.

The myth is full of profound and clear insight. The temptation offered to man is to "set up on his own", to be himself on his own terms, and to betray his managership of God's creation. It is, in human experience, an archetypal temptation. And it was (and is) accepted and fallen for.

The penalty is built into the act, and it is disastrous. But first to be condemned is the serpent, who is condemned to be earthbound (*Gen 3:14–15*). "The great dragon was thrown down, that serpent of old that led the whole world astray, whose name is Satan, or the Devil— thrown down to earth, and his angels with him" (*Rev 12:9*). And our Lord tells us, "I watched how Satan fell, like lightning out of the sky." (*Lk 10:17*.) Man suffers the inevitable, built-in consequence of his folly but the instigator—the tempter to whom man has in some way committed his will—is of another order of being altogether, and is deprived of his natural place in the scheme of things.

The traditional belief is that the Devil (Satan) is an archangel that has fallen through the sin of pride. There is reference in the New Testament to "the Devil and his angels" in more than one place, and demons are generally held to be fallen angels—of an order of being that is "other" but earthbound, a kind of malevolent, objective nothingness. St Augustine, in *The City of God*, tells us: "One (the angels) dwelling in the heaven of heavens, the other (the demons) cast thence, and raging through the lower regions of the air." Those that are "cast thence" rage through what we now recognise as the within of phenomenal creation, and in so far as they may be objectively perceived by man (as, very occasionally, they are), it is with his psychic sense and not his reason. Angels and demons, according to St Augustine, are "dissimilar and contrary to one another, the one both by nature good and by will upright, the other also good by nature but by will depraved" (*C. G. xi.33*).

An acknowledgement of the reality and place of such a being as a demon (or of Satan himself) makes it possible, perhaps, to perceive in some measure how an aberration within the volume, let us say, of a sphere might affect the circumference; or how the fall from grace of such a one as a Michael or a Gabriel could cause a smaller and weaker image of God to become deranged, and set nature's teeth and claws on edge until they ran red. The fall of a child in the nursery will, after all, cause the toy soldiers on the table to fall over and the fort to collapse.

We may become impatient of the orthodox Christian doctrine and wish that it spoke to our own generation in terms that are more fashionable. But in terms of human experience, "it works", and as far as Holy Scripture is concerned, it is faithful.

The idea of hierarchy in the demonic order is not a Christian one, although Christian writers have, from time to time, touched upon it, obtaining their material from other than specifically Christian sources. S. L. McG. Mathers, a bizarre but authoritative figure in Western occultism published *The Kabbalah Unveiled* in 1887 (the spelling of Qabalah varies frequently). This book, containing three of the books of the thirteenth-century Jewish *Zohar*, deals with the subject of "Qliphoth", or demons, in its introductory section. The idea of the four "worlds" archetypal, creative, formative and material, has already been considered in chapter six. "The fourth is . . . the world of action, called also the world of shells . . . which is this world of matter, made up of the grosser elements of the other three. It is also the abode of the evil spirits which are called 'the shells' by the Qabalah, . . . *Qliphoth*, material shells. The devils are also divided into ten classes, and have suitable habitations. The Demons are the grossest and most deficient of all forms . . . . The two first are nothing but absence of visible form and organisation. The third is the abode of darkness. Next follow seven Hells occupied by those demons which represent incarnate human vices, and torture those who have given themselves up to such vices in earth-life. Their prince is *Samael*, the angel of poison and of death. His wife is the harlot, or woman of whoredom, *Isheth Zenunim*; and united they are called the beast, *Chioa*. Thus the infernal trinity is completed, which is, so to speak, the averse and caricature of the supernal Creative One. Samael is considered to be identical with Satan."[1]

A number of these ideas are already familiar from other sources, and this is by no means a Christian understanding. But it is allied to the traditions from which some Christians have obtained their sources in the little that has been written on this most sorry of all subjects. We should note, however, that there is no question whatever of dualism. Satan is in no sense an "opposite number" of the Almighty. He is a kind of objective "absence of visible form and organisation"; a state, that is, of "having been an archangel", and obscenity—the perversion of Love and the hollow shell of its forms—is the character and keynote of evil. Though demons may enjoy such a measure of being as can be summed up in the expression "objective nothingness", and thus, although "evil spirits" may be said to exist, evil itself has no being. Evil, even at its most virulent, is no more that the willed and deliberate absence of good.

In the first chapter of Genesis, "the earth was a formless void, there was darkness over the deep" (*Gen 1:2*). God created Cosmos out of Chaos. W. G. Grey writes of these two principles in his *Magical Ritual Methods*. That the occultist's understanding of things is not the same as the Christian's, is, by now, plain. Nevertheless there are some important insights behind his thinking.

"Our Primal Life-Pattern should be clear enough . . . whether the Life-Pattern is expressed visibly, audibly, or by any means whatever, it remains what it is, COSMOS. The anti-Pattern is CHAOS. Its principle is the Many without One relative Constant. Electrons with no nuclei,

[1] S. L. McG. Mathers, *The Kabbalah Unveiled*, pp. 29-30.

planets with no Sun, hence sometimes miscalled the 'Forces of Darkness', implying intentional malignity . . . Since the Patterns of Chaos
do not have any recognizable formation that we can define in an ordinary
way, we are only able to identify them by their affect on humanity and
the results they produce. . . . As humans, our natural state is that of
Cosmos, and when we allow ourselves to live otherwise, or are caught
into Chaotic forces beyond our control, we get into trouble."[1]

The occultist's doctrine of God is inadequate, in Christian eyes. And
indeed, there seems to come into occult thought an idea of ultimates
"beyond God" because of this inadequacy. Thus Grey maintains:
"Cosmos and Chaos should not be confused with the Principles of what
we call Good and Evil in the sense of intentional malice or beneficence.
It is quite possible to work Cosmically with 'evil' intentions or Chaotically with 'good ones'. The main difference is that Chaotic evil is aimed
at breaking up the very basis of our Creation. It is always wise to choose
the lesser of these two. There is a very simple ruling to decide the
difference between Cosmic and Chaotic matters. Is the Divine Primal
Principle acknowledged and adhered to, or denied and abrogated?
The former is Cosmic, and the latter Chaotic. This does not mean the
profession of any kind of religion or belief in personal Deities. It
means whether the units of an Existence relate with each other via
their common Causative Spirit or not.

"The old notion of a Principle Evil Spirit who hated the Divinity and
all mankind was at least the concept of a Cosmic Devil who accepted
the existence of Deity. One cannot hate or love without establishing a
definite relationship between points of consciousness in Cosmos. That
is why it is important to make a Love-relationship between individual
entities and Deity Itself, since this makes a perfecting Cosmos. Our
chief need as souls is relationship between ourselves and all others in
the best possible way. Even bad relationships are preferable to Chaotic
incoordination. Better the Devil known than the Devil unrealised. A
Devil or Deity with which no relationship is possible for us as humans,
has no Cosmic validity for relative creatures like ourselves."[2]

The pre-Christian world-view is always mechanistic, and the

---

[1] W. G. Grey, *Magical Ritual Mods*, pp. 276–7.
[2] *Ibid.*, pp. 280–1.

occultist's version is even more so than most. The whole of creation is a piece of conscious machinery and the Creator is in some sense "within" it and identified totally with it. Thus, in a sense, God is at risk, for "We are up against a far greater menace to our Existence than Lucifer with his personal dislike of mankind. The real Companions of Chaos are utterly devoid of anything we would recognise as any kind of feeling. They are not really enemies in that sense at all, but Eliminators. Since to them Cosmos and its products, such as the human race, is an incompatible, Cosmos must either cease or be converted to Chaos. . . . It is the Cosmic Pattern of Life itself they mean to break, and if humans associate with it, then those humans must be dissociated into Chaos. No more nor less than that."[1]

Without accepting Grey's world-view, we may see in what he writes a clear picture of the patterns of Grace and sin. When, in Genesis, God ordered his Cosmos he "saw that it was good". Sin is destructive of that order and tends back towards Chaos, yet always within the Divine Providence. This is the great mystery with which I shall seek to deal in the next chapter.

[1] *Ibid.*, p. 281.

# 12

# By Divine Permission

It is a very difficult matter for men to take a deliberate step (mentally) out of his own environment. Time is our milieu, and Time seems to us to be an Absolute. It is, of course, nothing of the kind. To the human consciousness Time resembles a straight line, and its relationship to Eternity seems to be that of an endless piece of string in an abyss. Time is a kind of one-dimensional reality (to our minds) and there are no natural causes which would lead a conscious straight line—if such a concept may be imagined—ever to suppose the existence of other dimensions. The idea of area would be quite incomprehensible to a one-dimensional straight line. Mystical experience might convey a measure of "knowing" but such a transcendent experience could only be alluded to in terms of poetry. The totality of the square of which our straight line is a part—essential to the very "squarehood" of the square —is a two-dimensional reality wholly beyond the imagination, and outside the experience of a one-dimensional straight line, of whatever intellectual gifts.

But let us suppose that Reality—that sum total of things of which our straight line is a part—is not a matter of two dimensions, but of three. Supposing reality is a cube! How much further removed from linear comprehension is the concept of volume!

Now the human dilemma is akin to the light-hearted absurdity in which we have indulged. We talk about a time as a "fourth dimension", and mathematicians and physicists tell us that we live, move and have our being in the context of a multi-dimensional Space–Time continuum. And neither they nor we can be sure what is meant by this impressive phrase. But to talk of a multi-dimensional Space–Time continuum is to renounce the idols of Absolute Time and Absolute Space and acknowledge instead the immensity and unimaginability of things. At the same time that we acknowledge these, we are acknowledging the insights of mysticism. We can only think of Time in linear terms because Time presents itself to us as if it were eternally passing; we suppose that there must be an "end" but we cannot imagine it, and our efforts to do so involve us in great and disturbing unrealities.

What we may possibly describe as our linear theories about original sin and the fall are bound, therefore, to be inadequate and to comprehend only one dimension of the reality of any situation with which they seek to deal; In the image we began with—one edge of the cube.

Orthodoxy in Christian theology is that form of words, that statement of belief which enables human reason and divine Revelation to be most comfortably at ease with one another within our environmental limitations. Orthodoxy is always something of a knife-edge. It represents an acutely sensitive balance between apparently incompatible truths, each one of which, if taken in isolation, is an error! The orthodox Christian resembles nothing so much as a centipede; his stomach rests along the knife-edge and his every foot stands upon a different heresy! It is not a comfortable stance, but he cannot better it for the life of him.

If we are to be faithful to Revelation and take our Lord's words seriously, and thus recognise that Reality includes dimensions other than those with which we are familiar and can comprehend, then we must seek to come to terms with an understanding of the devil. We must seek to do that from which academic theology tends to shrink and deal with matters which human reason cannot comprehend other than in terms of poetry and myth. Part of our reluctance to come to terms with the problem of "the devil and his angels" stems from a very proper abhorrence of dualism, but we can be driven by our abhorrence into an unconscious monism if we are unwary. We can do no better than to be reminded that the devil (and his angels) is a creature of God like ourselves, although of a different order of being, and that the sin of Satan is identical with that of Adam—pride. Both have this in common, that each seeks to be "god" in his own right, and to exist on his own

D

terms. As an essential corollary, each seeks to make all other known beings his "creature". Both have fallen by virtue of that essential free-will which is inherent in a "son of God" (each according to his own order), and both are in a state of death because of this denial of the very basis of their own being. And yet they are, and shall forever remain—because God loves them!

Why did God not unmake man—and Satan—as soon as he sinned? The answer to this vexing question is that "God is Love", and Love is of the very essence of the nature of God and will not destroy what itself has created. The created free-will may, of its own volition, embark upon a course which leads back to Chaos, but Love will rather see the erring creature re-made (by the exercise of that same free-will, aided by Grace) through saving faith in the redemption wrought by the Incarnate Lord upon the cross. God, whose love is infinite, will restore his fallen creatures to Grace and Reality by the free exercise of that very faculty which led to their downfall.

There is all the difference in the world between pre-Christian and Christian theology. The monism of Hinduism, Buddhism and Western Occultism must inevitably present God's dealings with his creation as a mechanical process. Often the insights are very penetrating and most profound, and it would be a mind as unwise as it is arbitrary which would sweep them aside. The "working hypothesis" works and is validated by the experience of the persons holding to it. The important thing that must be determined is what it is all about, what the process is doing; but the Christian understanding of God's dealings with his creation does not depend, essentially, upon processes, but perceives a Divine state of mind. We may thus define Love as being the permanent state of the Eternal Mind. Processes abound in creation, but the state of the Mind of God transcends them all.

If God's nature is intrinsically as Christians understand it to be, must it not follow that another, fallen, rational creature of any other order of existence remains eternally loved? May it not be that Satan will be redeemed? We may ask these questions in all devotion and charity, but we must bear in mind the timeless nature of the angelic—and thus the demonic—order. Absolute Time and Absolute Space (our imagined milieu) are absurdities. For all we know a cosmic fall might have preceded creation as we know it!

As a fallen creature, the devil is undoubtedly loved by a saving and redeeming God; but he is unlikely to enjoy that love. His behaviour as tempter of mankind may, through our Lord's victory, be turned to good account. Despite his most malicious endeavours he may, at the End, be found to have been usefully employed to the Glory of God. In Longfellow's words:

> "Since God suffers him to be,
> He too is God's minister,
> And labours for some good,
> By us not understood."

We are left to conclude that the frustrations of Hell must be Hell indeed!

In the book of Job (which seeks to explain the sufferings of the innocent), Satan seeks permission of God to try Job's faith and see if it will endure adversity. He is given leave to go so far with his torments, but no further. Now this insight is crucial. Even in his sin, Satan can only go so far, and it is indeed as if he sins by divine permission! But having said this we must beware, for it is Satan's continued existence that is the subject of divine permission, and his activity is consequent upon his fallen nature; his activity is not permitted as activity. Intrinsic to both demonic and human make-ups are restrictions, and as the New Testament makes clear, man is not permitted to suffer more demonic assault than he can bear; God's grace is sufficient if man will only lay hold on it. The devil is by no means permitted to do that from which even God restrains himself; he may not over-ride the human will. At some stage, human integrity must surrender itself in order to sin; Satan cannot dominate it.

For man, a measure of torment is a means of grace. If there were no temptation to intemperance, who could call himself abstemious? If fornication were impossible, who could call himself chaste. If there is no temptation to steal, who can be honest? Moral choices must abound if man is to be human; options there must be on every side, and it is the peculiar frustration of Hell that, in seeking man's ruin, it gives him the means of sanctity! Heroic virtue could never manifest itself but for "the miseries of this sinful world". The calling of man is to conform his free will to the Will of God and this is a painful and lifelong struggle. Man, in the Christian view, must become what he is. His end-in-view is not a return to the Paradisal innocence, figured in the various "heavens" of monistic religious systems—the within of this world—but to total fulfilment and union with God.

There is another dimension to human suffering. We may be as pious and as devout as Job, and as complaisant! After all, he knew he was a good man! We may never take seriously the realities of our existence—and who can tell if Job's view of things was not superficial, at least to start with. Smug affluence feels no need of God; we may be the best of fellows and still perish. There is no way left, save catastrophe, of bringing home to the self-satisfied the awareness that God made him, that God is God and he is not. It is essential to the integrity of humanity that man should come to terms with reality at some time in his life and acknowledge, "God made me". If he never does, then he has never acknowledged the objective reality of his own existence. It is better that man should suffer than that he should perish, the infinite compassion of God demands it.

The rebellion of the devil and his angels, their corruption of the world, and the resulting sins of man are woes unutterable which, nevertheless, are turned back into the way of peace by the saving victory of the Christ. The pattern of recovery is important to note. The psychological recovery of a disturbed person is not a straight line inclining upwards. Rather, it is a series of levels, violent drops, followed by considerable advances, and a settlement at a new and higher level. This is the general pattern of all spiritual growth in an individual (which is a kind of recovery), and what is generally true for the one is true for the many. And so it is that a corrupted society with eroded moral standards, an increasing absence of direction or purpose, and a growing threat of anarchy, moves to the edge of a violent drop. Often there is a drop indeed, but after the nadir is passed, a better society at a new level will emerge. But sin matters; God is not glorified in anarchy and horror. "Alas for the world that such causes of stumbling arise! Come they must, but woe betide the man through whom they come!" (*Matt 18:7*)

It is important to remember the limitations imposed upon our understanding by the concept of Time, and of its seemingly one-dimensional aspect in a poly-dimensional whole. But for all this we must not lapse into a Monistic oblivion as to the significance of history, nor may we ignore the significance of evolution. Our Lord's Incarnation was both historical, and in the context of the evolution species as a whole and man in particular. Occultism seeks, with no great success, to reconcile emanationism with evolution and its theology proclaims both principles without convincingly uniting them. Monism cannot allow things to truly evolve because it is itself a static world-view, and the idea of the evolution of God, which is the monist's escape-hatch, makes it necessary to posit a "God beyond God" in some form or another.

Time matters; it is man's milieu. God's milieu is to us what the idea of volume is to a straight line. To God, all is NOW, but an attempt to comprehend God and creation by purely intellectual means will end in a sterile debate as to whether God did or did not create the best of all possible worlds!

The fall then was a pre-existent possibility if not—in some sense—a pre-existent fact. But so was its correction. Thus we understand the Cross to be a pre-existent fact which touches the human milieu in terms of history at Calvary, and thereafter throughout history upon the altars of the Church. The mind can boggle, but let us imagine that we are travelling upon the railway; we experience Worthing, Shoreham and Brighton as and when they appear outside our carriage window. But God sees the whole of Sussex at once, as an entirety. We observe the repairs to the railway bridge when we come to it, and we are thankful. But God repaired it, as it fell, on the day railways were invented, before ever we were born to begin our journey.

· · · · · ·

What may be described as the intellectual problem of evil and the Fall is essentially insoluble by mortal man in this life, if only because of the limitations—dimensional and environmental—already discussed. But we are not thereby absolved from making the best we can of the problem. Our theories must, by the very nature of things, sound rather like the base-fiddle part of an orchestral symphony. It is only when we have left the confines of our present, earthly condition that we shall hear the piece in its totality. Already, perhaps, we perceive the makings of harmony and counterpoint in things. When, as is to be desired, we get to heaven, we may be astonished by the very excellence with which our base-fiddle harmonises with the rest of the orchestra, and how totally God is glorified in us, and in the tune we are all playing.

# 13

# The Way things are

Man cannot conceive heaven, unaided. His consciousness must be expanded beyond anything that he can do for himself before he can comprehend anything approaching another dimension. Man can conceive neither the earth he inhabits nor his own self unaided. It is necessary that we step outside ourselves in order to see things as they are, and only from a point outside ourselves (not of our own choosing) will all the pieces of the human speculative jig-saw begin to promise an eventual coherent picture. Even this, like the picture on the jig-saw box, is a mere, sugary two-dimensional replica of the reality it seeks to convey.

It is important to stay with the concepts of the Fall and Original Sin a little longer, for it is these that lie at the heart of all human difficulties. At the Fall, man suffered a change of wavelength!

There have always been grave difficulties, and unrealities, attendant upon the attempts of man to come to terms with the fact that the Fall must, of necessity, have been historical in some way. For the reconciliation of the concept of an historical fall with the process of evolution of species which science reveals to us is very nearly impossible. As we have seen, all kinds of mental gymnastics are called for to reconcile human Reason with known, experienced—and, as Christians believe revealed fact. At best these exercises fail completely to satisfy. There is always a sense of unreality about something. At worst, they end by denying, either implicitly or explicitly, something that men know in their hearts to be true but prefer to abandon in order to balance their intellectual books. As related in Genesis, the Fall was indeed historical, but the present human understanding of Time makes it impossible for man to relate to it his own timescale and thus record it accurately in his books. And man has little patience with anything supposedly historical which cannot be fitted into history in a nice, orderly and reasonably comprehensible fashion.

The Australian Aborigines talk of the "Dream Time", and in so doing they give expression to a folk-memory of another world altogether. This is a universal phenomenon and is recorded in Genesis, not in the first chapter (which is pure theology), but in the very much more primitive second chapter, which is undiluted folk-memory.

"At the time when Yahweh God made earth and heaven there was as yet no wild bush on the earth nor had any wild plant sprung up, for Yahweh God had not sent rain on the earth, nor was there any man to till the soil. Yahweh God fashioned man of dust from the soil. Then he breathed into his nostrils a breath of life, and thus man became a living being.

"Yahweh God planted a garden in Eden which is in the east, and there he put the man he had fashioned . . . Yahweh God took the man and settled him in the garden of Eden to cultivate and take care of it. . . .

"Yawheh God said, 'It is not good that the man should be alone. I will make him a helpmate.' So from the soil Yahweh God fashioned all the wild beasts and all the birds of heaven. These he brought to the man to see what he would call them; each one was to bear the name the man would give it. . . ." (*Gen 2:5–20*)

It would be very difficult to find a general heading for the substance of this chapter better than the name given to it by the Aborigines of Australia; the "Dream Time".

The ancient text continues with the story of the garden of Eden to which we have already referred. Man disobeyed God's command; but the consequence of man's disobedience is highly significant:

"To the man he said, 'Because you listened to the voice of your wife and ate from the tree of which I had forbidden you to eat,

'Accursed be the soil because of you.
With suffering shall you get your food from it

Every day of your life.
It shall yield you brambles and thistles,
and you shall eat wild plants.
With sweat on your brow
shall you eat your bread,
until you return to the soil,
as you were taken from it.
For dust you are
and to dust you shall return.'

(*Gen 3:17–19*)

"So Yahweh God expelled him from the garden of Eden, to till the soil from which he had been taken. He banished the man, and in front of the garden of Eden he posted the cherubs, and the flame of a flashing sword, to guard the way to the tree of life." (*Gen 3:23–24*)

The whole nature of man's world is changed. From a god-like being he becomes an animal; his environment is wholly other, and—most significant of all—he is condemned to the condition of life which prevails on this other wavelength; "dust you are and to dust you shall return." Man is condemned to a cycle of birth and death.

The world man now inhabits is the same world, but on a different wavelength. His folk-memories of his innocent past remain and figure in his mythology, but he cannot relate them to his present circumstances. Plato, whose thinking I have discussed at least in parts, was referring in his concept of the Upper Plane as much to the unfallen wavelength as to a heaven of which he had virtually no conception. It was St John, not Plato, who related platonic concepts to heaven as we shall see in the next section. Man's present world is an imperfect and corrupted replica of the real world from which he fell. But it was a real earth man fell from—not heaven.

The world, indeed the Solar System, which man inhabits is largely a subjective one. His vision is limited to his own wavelength and thus he sees things as they appear on his wavelength and not as they are in themselves. The more he discovers about their apparent nature—on his wavelength—the more deluded he is likely to become as to their true nature. He thus perceives the Moon and the other planets of the Solar

System as they are on his wavelength, and not as they truly are; and in his ventures into Space, he lands upon a Moon as the Moon is on his wavelength. He does not know the Moon as the Moon is in itself. His perception of the very nature of Space itself is similarly limited.

Science has taught us a very great deal about the evolution of species on this wavelength, and that eminent thinker Pierre Teilhard de Chardin has related this process to the fulfilling process of redemption, and with others, has rendered a continuing warfare between science and religion ridiculous. But there is a missing link in all this; an enigma remains. It may very well have been the hand of Providence which caused Teilhard's religious superiors to inhibit his speculations about the Fall and Original Sin. The flow of his creative ideas might have been stopped or diverted into channels not yet ready for exploration. The time to think anew about the Fall was not then. It may, however, be the present. Teilhard's task was to resolve the then vexed questions concerning the relationship of Christian theology and the revealed process of evolution. In our own time, we may begin to perceive the relationship between the concept of the Fall as an historical fact and this same evolutionary process, a reality which can no longer be avoided. And in so doing, we may state the case as follows:

The Fall of man from a state of original innocence and grace was a moral inevitability consequent upon the existence, in him, of free-will. It was none the less culpable, however. When man fell, the whole process of the evolution of species in this wavelength was obliged to take place in order to evolve a creature for man to inhabit. Thus it may be said that the evolution of species as man understands it is a consequence of the Fall; but the correspondence of time-scales as between wavelengths is such as to make any human attempt at relating them meaningless. The Fall was, as we have said, inevitable but culpable, and we may best understand the workings of Divine Providence in this matter by recognising that evolution, on this wavelength, was prepared for man to fall into.

In an earlier chapter, we referred to the second account of the Fall which is recorded in the first four verses of the sixth Chapter of Genesis. The interpretation which we must now put upon this passage is very different from the one offered earlier, for this is, in fact, a folk memory of man's arrival on this wavelength.

"When men had begun to be plentiful on the earth, and daughters had been born to them, the sons of God, looking at the daughters of men, saw they were pleasing, so they married as many as they chose. Yahwch said, 'My spirit must not for ever be disgraced in man, for he is but flesh; his life shall last no more than a hundred and twenty years.' The Nephilim were on the earth at that time (and even afterwards) when the sons of God resorted to the daughters of man, and had children by them. These are the heroes of days gone by, the famous men." (*Gen 6:1–4*)

We may now possibly recognise "men", in this context, as the slowly evolved, innocent, Palaeolithic man, native to this wavelength; and "the sons of God" as being fallen, sinful men from another wavelength. We do not know how, when or in what manner such a fall took place. There are no history books. Man fell from Eden to the jungle and became identified with it wholly. The Nephilim (or "giants") may be identified with the Holy Angels.

The folk memory of the garden of Eden is by no means limited to the Hebrews. It is the common property of man, in various forms. The Hebrew contribution was, significantly, that of making it a theological statement, and a moral one at that. Plato gave expression to a similar concept and called it Atlantis. He clothed Atlantis in urban rather than rural forms, and the natural catastrophe which, according to legend, overtook Atlantis, is but another way of saying what the myth of Eden says. The exact nature of the Original Sin is known to no man. Like Eden, like the land referred to as the "Dream Time", Atlantis certainly existed as an historical fact, but on another wavelength. All these concepts are different subjective clothings for the same folk memory of the real world, of the unfallen wavelength, that from which man is now exiled and to which, in the old way, he can never now return.

*Part Three*

A Consideration of Heaven

# 14

# Above and Below

In the beginning God created the heavens and the earth. I have been at some pains to draw distinctions between these two orders of creation, and in particular to distinguish the within of earth from heaven. In the process I may seem to be hanging a great deal more upon that primitive, Hebrew metaphysical peg than it was designed to bear. I have talked much of the earth, and now I must talk of the heavens; but with what authority?

> "No one has gone up to heaven
> except the one who came down from heaven,
> the Son of Man who is in heaven."
>
> *(Jn 3:13)*

It is as well to acknowledge that scholars are in constant debate as to which sayings in the four canonical Gospels can be absolutely relied upon as *"ipissima verba"* of the Lord.

The three Synoptic Gospels (Matthew, Mark and Luke) are, in the main, firmly in the Jewish tradition which lays great stress upon morals and is careless of metaphysics. The Jews were concerned with the Person of God, the persons of men, and the moral, personal relationships between them. This was their great and indeed unique contribution as "God's Chosen People". But the writer of the Fourth Gospel (who can, with reasonable confidence, be identified with the Beloved Disciple) had a very much wider concern and addressed his work to the Hellenistic world in which the Platonic metaphysical concepts were, generally speaking, commonplace. He recognised that the basic human need is a metaphysical one rather than a moral one; man needs assurance, first and foremost, about existence, being, the meaning of life, its context, and the hope of eternity. From these metaphysical categories, the moral ones follow quite naturally. The Fourth Gospel is often called "the Mystical Gospel", and very aptly, for it interprets the great mystical experience of the Incarnation in terms of its metaphysical as well as its moral implications. And it is important to notice that, although St John presents his material in broadly Platonic terms, there are some very unmistakable corrections applied therein to the currently popular Platonism.

The keynote of the whole Christian Revelation is Salvation, Redemption, Restoration. The Incarnation of our Lord represented both a fulfilment and a rescue operation at one and the same time. We may begin, therefore, by asking ourselves what St John thought it necessary that men should be rescued from; and at once we discover a grim irony in his use of Hellenistic terms and thought-forms, because it is the Cosmos—the world—from which man needs to be rescued. To the Hellenistic world, this was a startling and rather shocking thought. The one thing that impressed the Greek thinker was the order of the universe. Cosmos was the opposite of Chaos. Science impresses modern man with its revelations of the order of things. The Chinese mystic Lao-Tse perceived a moral order in the universe some three hundred years before Plato:

> "The universe is everlasting.
> The reason it is everlasting
> Is that it does not live for self, but gives
> Its life to others by its transformation.
> Therefore can it long endure!"
>
> (*Tao Teh Ching*, 7)

And here is St John proclaiming the need for man to be rescued from such an ordered universe!

But St John deliberately applied a subtle meaning to the word Cosmos. This was not just "the world", but "the world of men and men's affairs". Cosmos, in this understanding, is synonymous not with order but with radical disorder. Cosmos and Chaos are very nearly identified.

Lao-Tse's vision was very close to this; so was that of Confucius, and so was that of the Buddha. The universe is in harmony, they all proclaimed; only man is deranged and disordered. The second verse of the epigram already quoted, gives Lao-Tse's advice to the wise man to order his own affairs after the order of the universe around him:

> "And so:
> The wise man places himself last
> And finds himself in the foremost place!
> Regards his body as incidental,
> And thus his body is preserved!
> Is it not because he does not live for self
> That his self attains perfection?"
>
> (*Tao Teh Ching 7*)

The fundamental sin of man is his denial of the true basis of his existence; thus in respect of the Second Person of the Blessed Trinity, the Word or "Logos" of whom Christians believe that

> "Through him all things came to be,
> not one thing had its being but through him,"
>
> (*Jn 1:3*)

it was, chaotically, the case that

> "He was in the world
> that had its being through him,
> and the world did not know him,
> He came to his own domain
> and his own people did not accept him."
>
> (*Jn 1:10–11*)

Indeed, the case was worse, even, than this; for to his disciples our Lord said

> "If the world hates you,
> remember that it hated me before you."
>
> (*Jn 15:18*)

And indeed;

> "Father, Righteous One,
> the world has not known you."
>
> (*Jn 17:25*)

What explanation does St John offer for this radically deplorable state of affairs? In the final summing-up of his first General Epistle, he states specifically that

> "We know that we belong to God,
> but the whole world lies in the power of the Evil One."
>
> *(1 Jn 5:19)*

Of this "Evil One", Satan or the devil, our Lord says, on the eve of the Passion:

> "I shall not talk with you any longer,
> because the prince of this world is on his way.
> He has no power over me,
> but the world must be brought to know that I love the Father
> and that I am doing exactly what the Father told me."
>
> *(Jn 14:30–31)*

And also that

> "Now sentence is being passed on this world;
> now the prince of this world is to be overthrown."
>
> *(Jn 12:31)*

The derangement of the Cosmos, the world of men, is due to the devil, the "prince of this world", and the whole "world" may be summed up in the Pauline terms: flesh, sin, law and death. Both St John and St Paul are agreed that natural, unredeemed man is inextricably bound up with a "world of men" which is radically disobedient to God, in denial of the ground of its own being, and thus set firm in the way of destruction. From his own resources, man has no remedy that he can apply. The Greek world was obsessed with the idea of corruption and the Jewish world suffered delusions of spiritual grandeur. Our Lord exposed the fantasy:

> "You study the scriptures,
> believing that in them you have eternal life;
> now these same scriptures testify to me,
> and yet you refuse to come to me for life!
> As for human approval, this means nothing to me.

Besides, I know you too well:
You have no love of God in you."
(*Jn 5:39–42*)

Many who did come to our Lord for life dared not come into the open
about it. When pressed, "they put honour from men before the honour
that comes from God" (*Jn 12:43*). It is ever the tragic delusion of man
that he imagines that he is "quite all right as he is".

I have already referred to the Platonic concepts of various planes of
being. To relate these specifically to the two orders of creation proclaimed at the beginning of Genesis is a simple and relatively obvious
exercise, for "the heavens" of Genesis relate to the "realm of forms
or ideas" in Plato—the Upper Plane upon which existence is wholly
real, perfect and unchanging. The "earth" in Genesis relates to the
Lower Plane in Plato, an imperfect reflection of the upper, and dependent upon it; upon which existence is derivative, imperfect, changing
and subject to corruption. In presenting his material specifically in
Platonic terms, St John was at once true to the basic Biblical metaphysic, and also perceived that a quite clear statement in metaphysical
terms must be made if our Lord's Person and ministry is to be properly
understood, and if the fundamental needs of man—metaphysical needs
before moral ones—are to be seen to be fulfilled in the Christian
revelation. Verbs and nouns which relate to "going up" and "coming
down" are in abundance, and our Lord could hardly have endorsed
this metaphysical framework more clearly when he said:

"You are from below;
I am from above.
You are of this world;
I am not of this world."
(*Jn 8:23*)

And while we must always remember that a metaphysical concept is
only a concept—a human attempt to comprehend the incomprehensible—the Platonic concept has considerable support, at least by
implication, in both Old and New Testaments.

.    .    .    .    .

The Upper Plane can roughly be described as the milieu of God. Life, Light and Love as objective Realities belong to this plane; indeed the Upper Plane IS Reality and Truth, and all existence is dependent upon the Existence of the Upper Plane. Man can only look to the Upper Plane for the source and meaning of true Life, Eternal Life and the fullness of Being. To this he must aspire or perish. Thus our Lord says:

> "My flesh is real food
> and my blood is real drink"
> *(Jn 6:55)*

He is referring to the realities of the Upper Plane as opposed to the shadows of mere bodily sustenance upon the Lower Plane.

The Greek concepts were mechanistic, however, and essentially impersonal. St John corrects this and shows that the reality is in fact a very highly personal one. He introduces the Jewish concept of Spirit (*not* in this context the Holy Spirit, third person of the Blessed Trinity and proclaims this as being of the essence of the Upper Plane.

> "It is the spirit that gives life,
> the flesh has nothing to offer.
> The words I have spoken to you are spirit
> and they are life."
> *(Jn 6:63)*

Spirit is an Upper Plane reality—indeed Spirit IS Reality, for our Lord says:

> "God is spirit,
> and those who worship
> must worship in spirit and truth."
> *(Jn 4:24)*

The whole burden of the great prologue to the Fourth Gospel is that the life of God the Word, second Person of the Blessed Trinity, the author of all orders of creation, belongs to the Upper Plane, and that the Word, who is in himself the whole Reality of that plane—who IS heaven in other words—descended in the fullness of his Reality to

the Lower Plane, the plane not of Spirit but of Flesh, and became
"enfleshed" (incarnate).

"The Word was made flesh,
he lived among us,
and we saw his glory,
the glory that is his as the only Son of the Father,
full of grace and truth."
*(Jn 1:14)*

Flesh can only produce flesh. The Lower Plane realities are derivative and can reach no higher. Only Reality can produce Reality.

"What is born of the flesh is flesh:
what is born of the Spirit is spirit."
*(Jn 3:6)*

Sinful man, man enmeshed in the chaotic Cosmos to which St John
refers can neither see God nor know him—not merely as a moral consequence, but as a metaphysical fact. There is no possibility by the
very nature of things, of bridging the gap from the shadow to the
Real. If the gap is to be bridged, then the initiative must come from
Reality.

Man is not an initiator; in particular he is not a self-initiator. He
receives his own being, he does not take it upon himself. Existence
is something that is undergone, but just as the life of the Lower
Plane is a thing received, so may also the Life of the Upper Plane be
received, through the initiative of him

"who was born not out of human stock
or urge of the flesh
or will of man
but of God himself."
*(Jn 1:13)*

Having thus established the metaphysical framework it is necessary
to attend to its implications in the matter of man's redemption.

# 15

# Bridging the Gap

Sin can be defined as an attitude of mind which seeks to exist upon its own terms, which attempts to attain to the "higher" life by its own unaided resources, which either ignores or seeks to minimise the gulf between the various planes of existence, and which supposes that man can bridge this gulf himself and wind himself up to Godhead, unaided. The technical name for this is Pride. A blindness to metaphysical reality is of the essence of sin; man is forever chasing after shadows and pretending to be what he is not. Our Lord exposes this complete unreality when he asks,

> "How can you believe,
> since you look to one another for approval
> and are not concerned
> with the approval that comes from one God?"
>
> *(Jn 5:44)*

When men seek "glory" from one another, they cut themselves off automatically from the real Glory—the Being of God himself in so far as man can perceive and know him. This is of the very essence of sin; it is the essential nature of that chaotic Cosmos from which, as St John saw so clearly, man is in desperate need of rescue.

Human approval, honour among men—earthly "glory"—is to be recognised for what it is; it is a counterfeit, and it is not to be sought for in place of the Reality. But it is as well to consider what is meant by "counterfeit". It is an imitation, a reflection, a derivation. It has its own integrity, but that integrity is outraged when it is taken to be the original from which it is derived. There is a very real sense in which we may regard the whole of the Lower Plane as a Divinely created counterfeit of the Upper Plane. But we must beware lest this

common usage of words leads us into an attitude of world-rejection;
of regarding this world as "mere illusion". It is of this world that, in
the best Christian tradition, Traherne writes: "Had I been alive in
Adam's stead, how I should have admired the glories of the world!
What a confluence of Thoughts and wonders, and joys, and thanks-
givings would have replenished me in the sight of so magnificent
a theatre, so bright a dwelling place; so great a temple, so stately a
house replenished with all kind of treasure, raised out of nothing and
created for me and for me alone. . . . How glorious must the King be,
that could out of nothing erect such a curious, so great, and so beautiful a fabric! It was glorious while new: and is as new as it was glorious."[1] And it was the "flesh" of the Lower Plane that Teilhard de
Chardin blessed in his *Hymn to Matter:*

> "Blessed be you, harsh matter, barren soil, stubborn rock: you
> who yield only to violence, you who force us to work if we would
> eat.
> Blessed be you, perilous matter . . .
> Blessed be you mighty matter, irresistible march of evolution,
> reality ever new-born . . .
> Without you, without your onslaughts, without your uprootings
> of us, we shall remain all our lives inert, stagnant, puerile, ignorant,
> both of ourselves and of God. . . ."[2]

Let us not, in our thinking of Upper and Lower Planes, become
rarified or precious; in both we are dealing with Almighty God, and
the Will of Almighty God made manifest.

I ended the previous chapter with the suggestion that, just as man
is in receipt of his being, and of his life upon the Lower Plane, so
might he also be in receipt of Eternal Life upon the Upper Plane if it
pleased God to bridge the gap and take the shadow up into the
Reality. This possibility is fulfilled in the Incarnation:

> "God's love for us was revealed
> when God sent into the world his only Son
> so that we could have life through him;

[1] Thomas Traherne, *Centuries*, p. 32.
[2] Teilhard de Chardin, *Hymn of the Universe*, pp. 68–69.

this is the love I mean;
not our love for God,
but God's love for us when he sent his Son
to be the sacrifice that takes our sins away."

(1 Jn 4:9–10)

This kind of initiative can only come from the Creator, it cannot come from the created;

"Yes, God loved the world so much
that he gave his only Son,
so that everyone who believes in him may not be lost
but may have eternal life."

(Jn 3:16)

Man, "lost" in the chaos that men call Cosmos, is rescued by adoption into Divine sonship! But the sonship of man is by adoption because man belongs, not to the Upper Plane by nature, but to the Lower. Yet man enjoys, in the legal sense of adoption deliberately used by St Paul, all the rights and privileges of the natural-born child. We have the "spirit of sons" (*Rom 8:15*), indeed.

"God sent his Son, born of a woman, born a subject of the Law, to redeem the subjects of the Law and to enable us to be adopted as sons. The proof that you are sons is that God has sent the Spirit of his son into our hearts: the Spirit that cries, 'Abba, Father', and it is this that makes you a son, you are not a slave any more; and if God has made you son, then he has made you heir" (*Gal 4:57*). St Paul was clear beyond doubt that the Divine initiative determined that "we should become his adopted sons, through Jesus Christ" (*Eph 1:5*). And in his great high-priestly prayer, our Lord prays thus for his adopted brothers and sisters:

"Father,
I want those you have given me
to be with me where I am,
so that they may always see the glory
you have given me
because you loved me
before the foundation of the world."

(Jn 17:24)

Jesus dwells, from eternity, upon the Upper Plane, a native, as it were, of the heavens. He possesses Glory in him by nature.

> "If I were to seek my own glory
> that would be no glory at all;
> my glory is conferred by the Father,
> by the one of whom you say, 'He is our God',
> although you do not know him."
>
> (*Jn 8:54*)

The Creed proclaims that the one Lord Jesus Christ, the only-begotten Son of God, "for us men, and for our salvation came down from heaven". This is a statement of plain fact, for the Incarnation (the "enfleshment") of the Word of God was in every respect the most profound "coming down". Our Lord did not "bring down" the fullness of the Divine consciousness, however; if a homely and naïve analogy be sought, he resembled somewhat an adult at a children's party! "The Word was made flesh, he lived among us" (*Jn 1:14*), and entered totally into the conditions, status and limitations of the flesh. Thus, "Jesus, tired by the journey, sat straight down . . ." (*Jn 4:6*) and said to the Samaritan woman he encountered, "Give me a drink". And again, at the death of Lazarus, "Jesus said in great distress, with a sigh that came straight from the heart, 'Where have you put him?' " (*Jn 11:33–35*) and then, "Jesus wept". At Gethsemane, "a sudden fear came over him, and great distress" (*Mk 14:33*); "in anguish he prayed even more earnestly, and his sweat fell to the ground like great drops of blood" (*Lk 22:44*). Our Lord, in his Incarnation, was fully human.

Flesh—the condition of the Lower Plane—has no life by its own right; it is wholly dependent and derivative; and in so far as he was Incarnate the Lord himself was dependent, as he made plain,

> "I, who am sent by the living Father,
> myself draw life from the Father
>
> (*Jn 6:57*)

But although dependent through the limitations of Incarnation, as the pre-existent Son he knew where he came from, knew God and had

seen God, and at times recalled into his human understanding his
Divine being:

> "Now, Father, it is time for you to glorify me
> with that glory I had with you
> before ever the world was."
>
> (*Jn 17:5*)

In the conditions of the Lower Plane, he continued to live the Life
of the Upper Plane, and this higher Life is to be understood as being
wholly identified with Love. As we have already heard;

> "The world must be brought to know that I love the Father
> and that I am doing exactly what the Father told me."
>
> (*Jn 14:31*)

and, by the same token,

> "my food
> is to do the will of the one who sent me,
> and to complete his work."
>
> (*Jn 4:34*)

Our Lord shared the Common Mind of Love with the Father, and the
expression of that Mind in the world was the way in which Jesus
showed his Love for the Father. The adopted sons of God are called
into participation in that same Common Mind:

> "I tell you most solemnly,
> whoever believes in me
> will perform the same works as I do myself,
> he will perform even greater works,
> because I am going to the Father."
>
> (*Jn 14:12*)

And later:

> "I tell you most solemnly,
> the Son can do nothing by himself;
> he can only do what he sees the Father doing;
> and whatever the Father does the Son does too.

> For the Father loves the Son
> and shows him everything he does himself."
> *(Jn 5:19–20)*

The implications for man are incalculable:

> "for the Father, who is the source of life,
> has made the Son the source of life."
> *(Jn 5:26)*

The Father has given the Son Life, not for himself alone, but for others too;

> "thus, as the Father raises the dead and gives them life,
> so the Son gives life to anyone he chooses."
> *(Jn 5:21)*

This gift of life is not, however, a simple, once-for-all gift which is made without regard to the way in which it will be used. It is morally conditioned; it is a continuous gift, which is continuously dependent upon continued identification with, and obedience to, the Father's will. To this we shall return in due course.

There is, as we have seen, a total unity of life-giving activity between the Father and the Son, for,

> "I do nothing of myself:
> what the Father has taught me
> is what I preach;
> he who sent me is with me,
> and has not left me to himself
> for I always do what pleases him."
> *(Jn 8:28–29)*

And in doing his Father's will in the bestowal of Life to man, our Lord affirms,

> "I give them eternal life:
> they will never be lost
> and no one will ever steal them from me."
> *(Jn 10:28)*

The total identification of Father and Son is affirmed again and again;

> "If I judge,
> my judgement will be sound,
> because I am not alone!
> the one who sent me is with me."
>
> *(Jn 8:15–16)*

"I am not alone" *(Jn 16:32)*, our Lord maintains, for

> "the Father and I are one." *(Jn 10:30)*
> "The Father is in me and I am in the Father."
>
> *(Jn 10:38)*
>
> "Father, I thank you for hearing my prayer.
> I knew indeed that you always hear me,
> but I speak
> for the sake of all these who stand round me,
> so that they may believe it was you who sent me."
>
> *(Jn 11:41–42)*

Such is the total identification of Father and Son; so totally has the gulf between the Upper and Lower Planes been bridged by our Lord's Incarnation that the man, Jesus, could say,

> "my word is not my own:
> it is the word of the one who sent me,"
>
> *(Jn 14:24)*

and, to the Samaritan woman at the well, he could say,

> "if you only knew what God is offering
> and who it is that is saying to you:
> Give me a drink
> you would have been the one to ask,
> and he would have given you living water."
>
> *(Jn 4:10)*

The categories of thought of Greeks and Jews were very different. The Hellenistic world thought in terms of the metaphysical categories—"seeing" and "being". The Jews thought in the moral categories—"hearing" and "obeying". But St John, the Jew, writing in Greek terms, introduces a category which transcends all these others

—a mystical category—that of "knowing". Jesus alone knows the Father, and he brings down with him the Divine glory.

> "Now has the Son of Man been glorified,
> and in him God has been glorified.
> If God has been glorified in him,
> God will in turn glorify him in himself."
>
> (*Jn 13:31–32*)

But Jesus does not merely bring down into the Lower Plane the Divine glory; he brings down the nature of God himself in terms accessable to man's understanding. In Jesus, man can know God! Men complain of anthropomorphisms in theological propositions, but in the Incarnation of the Divine Word, God himself perpetrated the ultimate anthropomorphism, deliberately and as the expression of an everlasting love. There was no bridging of the gulf, no adoption of men as sons of God in any other way. All who have eyes to see may see the glory of God in the person of Jesus;

> "To have seen me is to have seen the Father."
>
> (*Jn 14:9*)

The ability of Jesus to be the Son of God is morally conditioned by his continued obedience to the Father, and he is the bridge between the Planes, the "Jacob's Ladder" between heaven and earth, as he himself proclaims: "I tell you most solemnly, you will see heaven laid open and, above the Son of Man, the angels of God ascending and descending" (*Jn 1:51*).

> "God has given us eternal life
> and this life is in his Son;
> anyone who has the Son has life,
> anyone who does not have the Son does not have life."
>
> (*1 Jn 5:12*)

The gulf is bridged and manhood is, in the words of the *Quicunque Vult*, "taken into God", by the Incarnation of the Divine Word. Reality has produced reality in the midst of the shadow;

> "from his fulness we have, all of us, received—
> yes, grace in return for grace,

> since, though the Law was given through Moses,
> grace and truth have come through Jesus Christ."
>
> *(Jn 1:16–17)*

And, as our Lord proclaims;

> "I am the Way" (the reality, that is) "the Truth and the Life.
> No one can come to the Father except through me."
>
> *(Jn 14:6–7)*
>
> "I am the light of the world;
> anyone who follows me will not be walking in the dark;
> he will have the light of life."
>
> *(Jn 8:12 and 9:5)*

Jesus is the only possible light to illuminate and heal the Cosmos-in-chaos of the world of men. He is the bestower of both life and Life Eternal to man, in response to faith. Anyone who would have Life Eternal must look to Jesus for it, and to this end,

> "the Son of Man must be lifted up
> as Moses lifted up the serpent in the desert,
> so that everyone who believes may have eternal life in him."
>
> *(Jn 3:14–15)*

# 16

# Eternal Life

In Christ, the whole concept of the knowledge of God has advanced on to a new plane, and the fulfilment of our being is presented to us as the gift of the Life of the Upper Plane, the Life of Christ himself— in other words Eternal Life. And so, in this chapter, I shall refer much less to the metaphysical concepts. They are of human origin and it is well to remember this; they are attempts on the part of man to frame an understanding of that which is wholly "other" and beyond human understanding. They are the subjective response of human reason to mystical experience, and if they are allowed to become Absolutes, they turn into idols at once.

The gift of life in Christ is by no means unconditional. Indeed, it is morally conditioned—a continuous gift—and depends upon continued, willed identification in love with the Father's will and unconditional obedience to it. The relationship of the disciple with the Christ is similarly conditional upon obedience:

> "If anyone loves me he will keep my word."
> *(Jn 14:23)*

and, conversely,

> "Those who do not love me do not keep my words."
> *(Jn 14:24)*

The relationship of the disciple to Christ is analogous to that of Christ to the Father; as the Father works in Jesus, so the Christ works in the disciple; for, of the lover of Christ who keeps his words, our Lord says,

> "my Father will love him,
> and we shall come to him
> and make our home with him." *(Jn 14:23)*

The following definition of the Eternal Life can hardly be improved upon:

> "Father, the hour has come:
> glorify your Son
> so that your Son may glorify you;
> and, through the power over all mankind that you
>     have given him,
> let him give eternal life to all those you have
>     entrusted to him.
> And eternal life is this:
> to know you,
> the only true God,
> and Jesus Christ whom you have sent."
>
> *(Jn 17:1–3)*

Earlier, in his conversation with Nicodemus, our Lord had said;

> "Yes, God loved the world so much
> that he gave his only Son,
> so that everyone who believes in him may not be lost
> but may have eternal life."   *(Jn 3:15–16)*

Judgement and condemnation are to be understood as being "built in" to human free choice and are the lot which attends upon wilful refusal of the Life freely offered. Free-will, which is of the essence of man's nature, is respected to the bitter end! In his conversation with the Samaritan woman at the well, our Lord explains:

> "the water that I shall give
> will turn into a spring inside (a man)
>     welling up to eternal life."
>
> *(Jn 3:15–16)*

And, after healing the paralytic at the pool of Bethzatha, he says:

> "I tell you most solemnly,
> whoever listens to my words,
> and believes in the one who sent me,
> has eternal life;
> without being brought to judgement
> he has passed from death to life."   *(Jn 5:24)*

The response which is required from man is a simple one; he must accept Reality for what it is. Faith, in the Johannine sense, is simply seeing Jesus for what he is. It may be summed up, very simply, in the words, "Oh! I see!" There is nothing legalistic about the Johannine idea of faith, there is certainly nothing sentimental about it, and it might almost be said that there is nothing necessarily devotional about it either. Man just sees what IS, and he says "yes" to what he sees. He recognises Reality, and he walks thereafter in the light—and Life— of that Reality. To Martha, our Lord said;

> "If anyone believes in me, even though he dies he will live,
> and whoever lives and believes in me
> will never die." (*Jn 11:25–26*)

For, as the Prologue to the Fourth Gospel proclaims,

> "to all who did accept him
> he gave power to become children of God."
> (*Jn 1:12*)

The words and the works of Jesus were— indeed are—the means whereby the Life Eternal is mediated to man through the "flesh" of the Incarnate Christ. They are the challenge, the call to faith. The perception by man of the fact that,

> "The Father and I are one" (*Jn 10:30*)

is both a part of faith itself and also a reward of it. It is as one of the early Fathers of the Church once boldly asserted: "God became man in order that man might become God!"

St John, in the presentation of the Gospel, recognised the concepts and thought-forms of the contemporary Hellenistic world, and made full use of them. But he introduced into these concepts another, and one quite foreign to the thinking, not only of the Hellenistic world, but of virtually the whole pre-Christian world outside Judaism. This was the sense of the significance of time. St John saw the process in things, his was not the static world-view of the men of his day, for God is nothing if not dynamic, and there was, in the process of

E

redemption, a moment of ultimate importance. All through the Gospel there runs a thread of "not yet"; "My hour has not come yet", Jesus reminds his Mother at Cana (*Jn 2:4*). At the moment in Holy Week when Jesus specifically foretells his death and subsequent glorification, he cries;

> "Now the hour has come
> for the Son of Man to be glorified:" (*Jn 12:23*)

but it is worth remembering that, at the very Resurrection itself, he warns Mary of Magdala not to cling to him, "because I have not yet ascended to the Father" (*Jn 20:17*).

St John is very subtle in making the various "signs" of our Lord refer forward to the Passion. Thus the true cleansing of the Temple involves the death and Resurrection of the cleaner (*Jn 2:20–22*); the saving vision of which he spoke to Nicodemus involves "lifting up" (*Jn 3:14–15*); the true, life-giving water of which he spoke at the well in Samaria depends upon his suffering at the sixth hour (*Jn 4:6.10, 23 and 19:4*); and the true bread which is his flesh can be given only in death (*Jn 6:51*). Jesus raises the dead to life, but only at the cost of going to Jerusalem and dying himself at the hands of the authorities (*Jn 11:16 and 46*); and the Good Shepherd has to lay down his life for the sheep (*Jn 10:15*). For men, "there was no Spirit as yet because Jesus had not yet been glorified" (*Jn 7:39*).

There is abundant evidence that, for St John, the crucifixion is the moment of ultimate and eternal importance; the moment when the Life-giving Work is done. At the moment of death, our Lord said, "it is accomplished", and "gave up his spirit". This is to say, he made the Holy Spirit available for men! (*Jn 19:30*). And the blood and water which flowed from his pierced side is the "living water" (*Jn 4:10*), the "real drink" (*Jn 6:55*) of men adopted into sonship of the Father in Christ.

It will be worth our while to look, briefly, at St John's understanding of the death of Jesus. It was a result of the wicked council of men and the devil, but it was also the freely accepted and freely willed purpose of the victim, undertaken as an expression of love for the

Father, and on behalf of men (*Jn 10:17–18*). But, except for the Passion narrative itself, St John never speaks of crosses or crucifixions; he prefers to speak of our Lord "lifted up" or "glorified". Men brought Jesus utterly low, deprived him of any pretence of earthly "glory" by "lifting him up"; but he had always steadfastly renounced the "glory" of this world, and he had always sought only the true glory that comes from God the Father. And his seeking of it was the seeking of love, expressed in total obedience. Jesus was every inch a Jew in that he glorified God in the fullest Jewish sense by acknowledging both in word and in deed that God is the only and utterly sufficient source of salvation. The righteousness of Jesus consisted, in part at least, of his acceptance of the metaphysical reality. His trust was vindicated, and he was raised up to share again the primal glory of God.

God glorified the Son in his death. Because of his obedience to the Father, his "lifting up" by men was a lifting up indeed! Jesus reigned from the Cross. The crucifixion was the glorification. But there was more to it, even, than this: by submission to death and disgrace—the whole character of this Cosmos-in-chaos—when the ruler of the world had no claim upon him, he overthrew Satan and cast him forever out of power over the world.

This, in a nutshell, sums up St John's understanding of the Passion, but it is not quite a complete summing-up, because our Lord's victory was not, in St John's eyes, a solitary one. Our Lord always referred to himself as the "Son of Man". He was, and is, the True Self of the human race. As he now stands in the presence of God, so also may we in him.

> "I am in my Father
> and you in me and I in you;" (*Jn 14:20*)
> "He who eats my flesh and drinks my blood
> lives in me
> and I live in him." (*Jn 6:56*)

His going away is for our benefit (*Jn 13:33. 14:28*), for,

> "when I am lifted up from the earth,
> I shall draw all men to myself." (*Jn 12:32*)

In the lifting up of Jesus upon the Cross, the decisive Work is done, and the whole of humanity is lifted up on to the Upper Plane.

Men can share in this Eternal Life only in so much as they are in Christ. The life was not available for men before Christ was lifted up, but in his lifting up, he passed beyond all limitations—and so may we, in him. It was the widening of his contacts beyond the narrow confines of "God's chosen people" that enabled Jesus to proclaim, "now the hour has come". This fact is not without significance, and to it we shall return in a later chapter. Through faith, and Baptism, a relationship with Jesus can be established; "because I live, ye shall live also" (*Jn 14:19 AV*), and that relationship is corporate in character.

> "I am the vine,
> you are the branches.
> Whoever remains in me, with me in him,
> bears fruit in plenty;
> for cut off from me you can do nothing.
> Anyone who does not remain in me
> is like a branch that has been thrown away
> —he withers;
> these branches are collected and thrown on the fire,
> and they are burnt." (*Jn 15:5-6*)

The mutual indwelling of the Christ and the disciple both assumes and demands a life of Christlike quality, which is effected by the work of Divine Grace in the soul. The Christ and the Holy Spirit live and abide in Christians, but always and only through their identification with the one who has Life, and who stands in the presence of the Father. To abide in Christ, to see him and to know him, is to abide in the Eternal Life of the Holy Trinity. This, in a word, is heaven.

I took, as the title of this section, "A Consideration of Heaven", and in this consideration, aided by St John, I have transcended the metaphysical categories both of Plato and of Genesis. I have arrived, not at a metaphysical proposition, but at a living personal relationship. In the first two sections of this book I have been at some pains to draw a distinction between the earth, the within of earth and "the heavens".

But so far from arriving at the idea of a "three-tier universe" which popular thinking inclines to suppose, or even a "two-tier universe" which a superficial reading of Genesis might suggest (or of Plato, for that matter), we perceive that the whole of creation, the world, its within and its without, all archetypes, all forms, all ideas, realities, "principalities and powers", are all in God. And, utterly transcending every plane, every level, and indeed every conceivable category of being, is that personal relationship with God, in Christ, which we call Eternal Life. This is the Life of Christ, and this, for man at any rate, is heaven.

# 17

# A Proposal of Marriage

"Today," wrote C. G. Jung, "we talk of 'matter'. We describe its physical properties. We conduct laboratory experiments to demonstrate some of its aspects. But the word 'matter' remains a dry, inhuman, and purely intellectual concept, without any psychic significance for us. How different was the former image of matter—the Great Mother—that could encompass and express the profound emotional meaning of Mother Earth. In the same way, what was the spirit is now identified with intellect and thus ceases to be the Father of All. It has degenerated to the limited ego-thoughts of man; the immense emotional energy expressed in the image of 'our Father' vanishes into the sand of an intellectual desert."[1]

Man is the creator of his own deserts; things do not cease to be what they are because man has blinded himself to their nature, and the archetypal concepts of the Great Mother and the Father of All go very deep. No less venerable is the concept of the marriage of the "earth-Mother" with the "sky-Father", and the constantly recurring miracle of birth, death and re-birth; the fertility of crops and cattle and human beings was universally related, by primitive man, to such a concept. Sympathetic magic, the rituals of "sacral kingship" by which the fertility myths were re-enacted year by year, and the worship of male and female deities (including, through Canaanite influence, "consorts" for Yahweh at various times) sought to give expression to these deeply seated instincts, and at the same time to ensure the effective continuance of the reproductive miracle. The "old gods" have an objective reality; they are fundamental archetypes of creation. They were invested, by man, with various subjective realities as well, under various names. But a comparison of pantheons reveals a very

[1] C. G. Jung, *Man and his Symbols*, pp. 94–5.

ready identification of "god-functions" to which the appropriate local name can be applied. Thus the objective archetype was venerated, subjectively, as a "god" and invoked by many traditions under many different names. The ancients found little difficulty in the mutual identification of Pantheons. But the functions of sky-Father and earth-Mother were on a somewhat higher level than those of the various other deities. Claud Chavasse, in an important but neglected book' *The Bride of Christ*, quotes E. O. James and Rudolf Otto on the subject of the universal belief in tribal All-Fathers. "These shadowy All-Fathers have been obscured by the more intimate spirits, totems, and deified ancestors, but nevertheless they are now known to exist in the background of almost every primitive community . . . Belief in them . . . is the expression of an emotion, not the elaboration of a certain kind of knowledge about (the universe). . . . This universal mono-theistic tendency . . . is an emotional evaluation of what Otto would describe as *mysterium tremendum*, in the intuitive rationalisation of a Power, awful and mysterious, as the ground of the visible order."[1] Chavasse suggests that Abraham, on leaving Ur of the Chaldees, left behind the great city gods (identified with the powers of heaven) and took with him only his own family god, who thus became God, the "God of Abraham and Isaac and Jacob", a god of people rather than of places. He points out that, "certainly when Moses once more introduced monotheism to the temporarily enslaved Israelites, it was under this Abrahamic tradition that he did so. God said to him: 'Thus shalt thou say unto the children of Israel, Yahweh, the God of your fathers, the God of Abraham, of Isaac, and of Jacob, hath sent me unto you' (*Exod 3:15 AV*). It is a reversion to a half-forgotten All-Father. . . . Now, it is just here, in this divine revelation to Moses, a revelation which is a true revelation because it is 'the coincidence of divinely guided events and a mind divinely illumined' (E. O. James), that we can find the first source of the true nuptial idea. For it is here that we find God choosing the Chosen People and binding them in a Covenant of protection and obedience."[2]

· · · · ·

1 Claud Chavasse, *The Bride of Christ*, pp. 20–1.
2 *Ibid.*, pp. 22–3.

The nuptial idea, the marriage of heaven and earth, seems somewhat removed from the Fourth Gospel, and might seem, at first sight, to have little to contribute to this consideration of heaven. But this is very far indeed from being the case, for the nuptial idea is one of the most central ideas of all in the Old Testament, and is fulfilled completely in the New. What Chavasse has called the true nuptial idea is very different in character, however, from the myth-enactments and sympathetic magic of the pagan world, much of which had become deeply corrupted; the Bridegroom was Yahweh, and the Bride was— not "matter" or "the earth" or even "creation" as such—but Israel, the People of God. (To be more accurate, it is better to identify the Bride with the Shekhinah, the archetype of the People of God.)

The Prophet Hosea is the one who, more than any other, "is responsible for bringing into consciousness the essentially nuptial character of the nexus between Yahweh and Israel, the Choosing God and the Chosen People. In his case the relations between Yahweh and Israel are illustrated from the painful experiences of his own married life."[1] Hosea had married a wife who had borne him a son and a daughter, but who was constantly unfaithful to him. His own reaction, in redeeming and restraining and then restoring his wayward spouse, was used by him as an allegory of the loving correction by Yahweh of the unfaithful Israel. "Here then, in the very beginning of the literary prophets, we find the marriage idea fully developed. Yahweh is the Divine Husband; Israel is his Bride; their union is consummated in sacrifice; the unfaithfulness of Israel is adultery and fornication. So prominent a place does this idea of 'allegory', take in the writings of the prophets that it may be asked whether irregular sexual intercourse did not first appear immoral because it was like infidelity to Yahweh, rather than that infidelity to him was condemned because it was like adultery and fornication. At any rate it is quite evident that the notion of God the Husband is anterior to that of God the Father, of which it is the natural concomitant. It was also more natural to the Hebrew, whose idea of the nexus with his God was national and corporate and not personal."[2]

---

[1] Claud Chavasse, *The Bride of Christ*, pp. 28–9.
[2] *Ibid.*, p. 29.

Hosea, to whom the "sacred marriage" rituals of his time, with their orgiastic manifestations, were repellent, is thus the very one who most strongly underlines the true nuptial idea. A later one was Jeremiah, the great antagonist of the cult of the "Queen of Heaven".

"In the days of King Josiah, Yahweh said to me, 'Have you seen what disloyal Israel has done? How she has made her way up every high hill and to every spreading tree, and has prostituted herself there?" (*Jer 3:6*). The references are to the sacral marriage rites of the surrounding "gods". "I thought: After doing all this she will come back to me. But she did not come back. Her faithless sister Judah saw this. She also saw that I had repudiated disloyal Israel for all her adulteries and given her her divorce papers. Her faithless sister Judah, however, was not afraid: she too went and played the whore." (*Jer 3:7–8*.)

Ezekiel too, in exile, developed the Divine Husband theme and saw Jerusalem as a foundling, an outcast whom God adopts as his bride. Again, the bride plays the harlot and Ezekiel uses this idea to expound an allegory of God's punishment meted out in the tribulations of recent history. His language is fierce, but in the end: "I am going to renew my covenant with you; and you will learn that I am Yahweh, and so remember and be covered with shame, and in your confusion be reduced to silence, when I have pardoned you for all you have done—it is the Lord Yahweh who speaks." (*Ezek 16:62–63*.)

Ezekiel returned to the nuptial theme in chapter 23, but the Exile itself was seen, generally, as the chastening of the unfaithful Bride, and by the time the last section of Isaiah came to be written the Marriage of Yahweh and Israel is seen as a matter of pure and unmitigated joy:

> "I exult for joy in Yahweh,
> my soul rejoices in my God,
> for he has clothed me in the garments of salvation,
> he has wrapped me in the cloak of integrity,
> like a bridegroom wearing his wreath,
> like a bride adorned in her jewels."     (*Isa 61:10*)

In the chapter which follows, the Bride is addressed thus:

> "You are to be a crown of splendour in the hand of Yahweh,
> a princely diadem in the hand of your God;

> no longer are you to be named 'Forsaken',
> nor your land 'Abandoned',
> but you shall be called 'My Delight'
> and your land 'The Wedded';
> for Yahweh takes delight in you
> and your land will have its wedding.
> Like a young man marrying a virgin,
> so will the one who built you wed you,
> and as the bridegroom rejoices in his bride,
> so will your God rejoice in you." (*Isa 62:3–5*)

In the last chapter of Isaiah, Israel is, somewhat confusedly, identified with the Great Mother and thus there is a connection in thought between the People of God and Creation as a whole; Israel being the "consciousness" which is to enter into union with God.

But in the great nuptial psalm 45, a marriage-ode (which might conceivably owe its origin to the marriage of Ahab to Jezebel!), there is to be seen the beginnings of a "transference of the role of Bridegroom from Yahweh to the Messiah".[1] This is less clear in the psalm than in the interpretation of it which became common at a later date. This transference of role from the Father to the Divine Son continues, however, from the Old Testament to the New. Thus St John the Baptist, questioned about the activities of Jesus, said:

> "The bride is only for the bridegroom;
> and yet the bridegroom's friend,
> who stands there and listens,
> is glad when he hears the bridegroom's voice.
> This same joy I feel, and now it is complete."
>
> (*Jn 3:29*)

Chavasse remarks: "The interest here lies in the casual way in which the subject is introduced, not as anything new, but as a normal concept of the office of Messiah. It seems indifferent to the Baptist whether he said 'I am not the Christ' or 'I am not the Bridegroom'."[2] John clearly regarded his own baptism as being merely preparatory, but that of Christ as the beginning of the Nuptial Ceremonies themselves. In this

---

[1] Claud Chavasse, *The Bride of Christ*, p. 36.
[2] *Ibid.*, p. 50.

connection, it is interesting to reflect upon John the Baptist's reference to himself as "the bridegroom's friend". In contemporary Judaea there were two such "friends", one acting for the Bride and one for the Groom. They were responsible for all arrangements, negotiations, legalities and so forth. They were guarantors of the bride's virginity and they conducted the couple to the bridechamber. St John the Baptist evidently regarded himself as combining both functions within himself in respect of the Heavenly Bridegroom and Israel, the chosen Bride.

A concept is but a concept—a man-made, man-conceived thing. It is subjective, but there lies behind it an objective reality which it seeks to enshrine in terms comprehensible to men. This is manifestly the case with the concept of the Bridegroom and the Bride. There is a most fundamental, objective reality behind it, and the nuptial idea is no mere convenient mode of expression. Our Lord's own endorsement of it, casually and as a matter of course, is proof enough of that.

It is time, therefore, to examine the Gospel evidence in this connection, first the Synoptic Gospels, and then the Fourth Gospel; and thereafter to examine the nuptial idea in the Pauline Epistles and Revelations. For all these examinations I shall be in the debt of Claud Chavasse.

# 18

# Solemnisation of Matrimony

Eternal life, "heaven" that is, in so far as man is concerned, is to be identified with a personal relationship with God in Christ. And I am only interested in concepts, metaphysical and moral, which can explain something of the nature of that relationship. The nuptial idea, therefore, is of no consequence unless it does this.

The marriage customs of Palestine in our Lord's time cannot be reconstructed with complete accuracy, but the customs of the East in general, and of the Near East in particular, are both exceedingly ancient and remarkably similar. It is a reasonable assumption, therefore, that the pattern of events was somewhat as follows:

First of all came the Betrothal. This corresponds to our present-day idea of Engagement, but it was, to the Jew, legally binding. A betrothal could only be broken by divorce, even though the marriage had not yet been publicly solemnised nor consummated. Thus Mary was, in this very formal sense, engaged to Joseph when she was found to be with child through the Holy Spirit (*Matt 1:18–22*) and it was the termination of this legally binding engagement that Joseph contemplated. A betrothal was a firm promise of marriage. It was not the marriage itself.

Our Lord's Baptism, an utterly bewildering event to John the Baptist (*Matt 3:13ff*), is only really explicable if it is understood as our Lord's Betrothal to Israel—and through Israel to creation as a whole. It is his firm promise of union with his People, and through his people with "all men" (*Jn 12:32*) and with creation through mankind. A baptism of repentance is meaningless to one who needed no repentance, as every Gospel story indicates. Our Lord takes over the rite as his expression of formal betrothal, he to the world in the Jordan, and the world to him in the fonts of his Church. No other explanation of the Baptism in the Jordan is sufficient on its own.

"Three days later there was a wedding at Cana in Galilee. The mother of Jesus was there, and Jesus and his disciples had also been invited." (*Jn 2:1.*) The Marriage Feast was the time of solemnisation of the marriage. The bridal pair proceeded to the consummation of their marriage from the feast, and to our Lord, fresh from his Betrothal, with all that this implied to his own understanding, the village wedding must have been a poignant reminder of his own high nuptials that were yet to come. His mother's anxiety about the supply of liquid refreshment was a reminder, perhaps, of the unpreparedness of his Bride, of her infidelity. His reply was more of a meditation aloud than a direct answer to Mary. "Woman, why turn to me? My hour has not come yet." (*Jn 2:4.*) The "woman" was not Mary herself, but the Bride, Israel, of whom in some way Mary was a "summing up" just as she was, in some way, a personification of the "earth mother", whose own motherhood was the fruit of a marriage of "sky-father" and "earth-mother" of which the myths of the surrounding world were but shadows of the reality. Certainly Mary saw no rebuke in her son's remark, for she "said to the servants, 'Do whatever he tells you'" (*Jn 2:5*). She knew her Son.

Throughout the Gospels, and in the Synoptic Gospels particularly, our Lord assumes, almost casually, the role of Bridegroom. He does not say, "I am the Bridegroom" because he does not have to. Of course he is the Bridegroom if he is indeed the Saviour! He rebukes Israel for being an "adulterous and sinful generation . . . ashamed of me and of my words" (*Mk 8:38; Matt 12:39; 16:4*). He speaks of "the kingdom of heaven" being "compared to a king who gave a feast for his son's wedding" (*Matt. 22:2*), and he does this the day after his triumphal entry when, as both St John and St Matthew tell us, he rode into Jerusalem in deliberate fulfilment of the prophesy which begins:

> "Say to the daughter of Zion, 'Look,
> your saviour comes,'" (*Isa 62:11*)

"Rejoice heart and soul, daughter of Zion!
Shout with gladness, daughter of Jerusalem!
See now, your king comes to you." (*Zec 9:9*)

The "king" was the Bridegroom and the "daughter of Zion" the Bride. The context of the prophesies themselves make that clear beyond any doubt.

Earlier in his ministry, our Lord tells enquirers why his disciples do not indulge in penitential practices like those of John the Baptist: "Surely the bridegroom's attendants would never think of fasting while the bridegroom is still with them." (*Mk 2:18*.) And in the pharisee's house, he says; "When someone invites you to a wedding feast, do not take your seat in the place of honour!" (*Lk 14:8*.) Typically, human nature being what it is, at the Last Supper itself "a dispute also arose between them about which should be reckoned the greatest!" (*Lk 22:24*.) We shall consider in a moment the nuptial nature of that Last Supper, but in the context of Holy Week again, our Lord tells the parable of the wise and foolish virgins who "went to meet the bridegroom" (*Matt 25:1*).

The "bridegroom's attendants" that we have referred to were "simply a bridegroom's bachelor friends before his marriage. In the afternoon before the wedding the bridegroom used to leave his house, which was then occupied by the bride, and her attendants; meanwhile he sat among his companions. These were the 'sons of the bride chamber.' At a signal from the bridegroom he and his companions moved off slowly and ceremoniously towards his home, where the bride was awaiting him and where the bridal feast was to be held."[1] "It does not seem too much to claim that our Lord, in the Last Supper was as much enacting a Marriage Feast as keeping the Passover. Essentially the Passover itself was nuptial. The foundation of the Marriage beyween Yahweh and his people was the Covenant between them. That Covenant was made and ratified by the Passover. It is therefore no playing with words, but the sober truth, to say that Jesus, if not enacting a marriage at the Last Supper, was solemnising

[1] Claud Chevasse, *The Bride of Christ*, pp. 54-5.

the Marriage between himself and his Church in this, the New Covenant."

"Outwardly, too, the ceremonies of the Last Supper suggest a marriage of those days. The house was prepared as for the reception of the bridegroom who had absented himself with his friends; at a given signal, he and his party returned to find the room prepared for the wedding feast. The feast itself began with the prescribed hand-washing and benediction. Then the great winecup was filled, and the principal personage, taking it, and holding it, recited over it the prayer of bridal blessing. Only the men sat at the marriage supper. After the supper the bridegroom left the feast with the bride."[1] "Come now, let us go"; said our Lord to his Bride (*Jn 14:31*).

"It has caused much speculation," says Chavasse, "that our Lord at the Last Supper said, not 'This is my Flesh', but 'This is my Body'. The normal complement of blood is not body, but flesh, as we find in the sixth chapter of St John. But a bridegroom dedicates not his flesh but his body to his bride. 'With my body I thee worship' may not be the words of the Jewish Wedding Service, but the sentence enshrines a central idea of Christian marriage."[2] Just as, for St. John, the crucifixion of our Lord is his glorification, so the crucifixion sums up all the nuptial imagery of the Old Testament which, in Chevasse's words, "converge and meet on Good Friday". Our Lord's death was the consummation of the marriage. But the word is not *was*, but *is*. And from that moment, while time lasts, redeemed man, the Bride, betrothed at the font, and partaking of the marriage feast at the altar is called to realise, in the life of Grace, the potential within him, and become what he is, a member and part of the Bride of Christ which is both an individual and corporate reality for him. The most common image of the Church is the "Body of Christ", but she is only the "Body" by virtue of being the "Bride" for, as our Lord made clear, a man and his wife are "one flesh", an inseparable unity. So, in consummation of his marriage, the "death" which every consummation

---

[1] *Ibid.*, pp. 60–1.
[2] *Ibid.*, pp. 63–4.

involves becomes the source of life, and the Life in this case is the Eternal Life of Christ.

The nuptial idea was central to St Paul's vision. Basing his theology on the Genesis myths of creation, and of the essential identity of man and woman therein (Christ being the "new Adam" in this sense), he speaks constantly of the Church as Christ's body.

"There is one Body, one Spirit . . . There is one Lord, one faith, one baptism." (*Eph. 4:4–5.*)

"It makes me happy to suffer for you . . . to do what I can to make up all that has still to be undergone by Christ for the sake of his Body, the Church." (*Col. 1:24.*)

"May the peace of Christ reign in your hearts, because it is for this that you were called together as parts of one body." (*Col. 3:14.*)

"Now you together are Christ's body; but each of you is a different part of it." (*1 Cor. 12:27.*)

The idea of the Church as the "Body of Christ" is central to St Paul's doctrine, but "She is only the Body of Christ because she is primarily the Mystical Bride of Christ."[1] And perhaps the clearest expressions of this doctrine are to be found in two passages, one addressed to the Christian community in Corinth, and the second to that in Ephesus. In a spirit of rebuke, Paul writes to the erring and wayward Corinthian congregation thus:

"You see, the jealousy that I feel for you is God's own jealousy: I arranged for you to marry Christ so that I might give you away as a chaste virgin to this one husband." (*2 Cor 11:2.*) And to the Ephesians, he writes:

"A man never hates his own body, but he feeds it and looks after it; and that is the way Christ treats the Church, because it is his body— and we are its living parts. For this reason, a man must leave his father and mother and be joined to his wife, and the two will become one body. This mystery has many implications; but I am saying it applied to Christ and the Church." (*Eph. 5:29–32.*)

· · · · ·

[1] Claud Chevasse, *The Bride of Christ*, p. 71.

Chevasse described the Apocalypse of St John as "The Drama of the Victorious Bridegroom." Certainly every archetypal image relevant to the nuptial idea is present in St John's vision. But we need only concern ourselves with the final consummation of all things, which is described as the Marriage of the Bride to the Victorious Bridegroom.

"I seemed to hear the voices of a huge crowd, like the sound of the ocean or the great roar of thunder, answering, 'Alleluya! The reign of the Lord our God Almighty has begun; let us be glad and be joyful and give praise to God, because this is the time for the marriage of the Lamb. His bride is ready, and she has been able to dress herself in dazzling white linen, because her linen is made of the good deeds of the saints.' The angel said, 'Write this: Happy are those who are invited to the wedding feast of the Lamb.' " (*Rev 19:6–9.*)

# 19

# Finding the Words

Happy are those, the angel said, who are invited to the wedding feast of the Lamb. It is clear that this wedding feast and all it implies is of the very essence of the "heaven" that we are trying to consider and come to terms with. Heaven, for man, is a personal relationship with God in Christ; it is among other things a participation both in the Life and in the Mind of Christ. The heavenly marriage, the nuptial idea, tell us something of both the style of that identification, and also the degree. But if we would do justice to the concept of the wedding feast, we must approach it from another angle as well; we must spend a little time learning a language, an understanding of which is fundamentally necessary if we are to understand our Lord and his work. This language is the language of sacrifice.

Sacrifice is fundamental, not only to worship but to the whole of life. It is a principle built into creation because it is of the nature of God himself. To modern man, sacrifice is a remote concept—as far as worship is concerned at any rate. There are few people who have not participated in a wedding, but there are fewer still, in present-day Western society, who have participated in a sacrifice in the Old Testament, religious sense of that word. But our Lord used sacrificial language and fulfilled every sacrificial principle in his own being, and so we must return to the Old Testament in order that we may better comprehend the New.

Among the Hebrews of the Old Testament, the sacrificial observance followed two main patterns. Which one depended upon what was being expressed, for it is important to understand that by the offering of sacrifice, the offerer was giving expression to a state of affairs. He was expressing the relationship that he believed to exist between himself and God.

The first type of sacrifice was the Peace Offering. The victim was an animal, physically perfect, taken from the offerer's own flock or herd. It was offered as the representative not only of the offerer but of his whole household, their possessions, and their livelihood. Its offering was an acknowledgement of absolute dependence upon God, not only for livelihood but for very existence. It was an acknowledgement of reality. The sacrifice was not made lightly; the best animal was a costly beast, and the sacrifice was a sacrifice indeed. It represented the giving back to God of the whole of "self".

The offerer, the head of the family, brought the animal to the altar and, in the presence of the priest, laid his hand upon it and thus identified it with himself and his family. He then "gave it to God" by the simple process of cutting its throat.

The early Hebrews were innocent of scientific discovery, and as, by observation, a total loss of blood meant a total loss of life; blood and life were identified either with other. But life belongs exclusively to God, it is a part of his great mystery, and so the blood was collected in a basin by the priest and was sprinkled on and about the altar. (*Lev 3 et seq.*) Only God's priest could handle the blood, but the flesh was cut up and divided according to custom and the Law, and a great feast was held round the shrine. The meat was shared between the offerer, his household, the priest—and God. For "God's Portion" was burnt upon the altar while the feast was in progress.

The Peace Offering represented the expression of a right relationship existing between God and man; the relationship of the Covenant whereby "I will adopt you as my own people, and I will be your God." (*Exod 6:7.*) God and his people shared a common meal, each as it were in his proper place. It is a matter of universal experience that the sharing of a common meal is an expression—the main expression—of peace between those sharing. The Peace Offering was, in fact, exactly what its name implies.

The giving of offence, the denial of a human relationship by its wilful repudiation either by word or deed, destroys that relationship effectually even though it may not destroy it actually. This is tragically obvious in cases of marital dispute or in family quarrels. The relationship *is*, and nothing can alter that fact, but effectually it is ruptured and is as good as destroyed. The injured party must be willing to forgive but the offender must make himself forgivable by seeking and accepting such forgiveness. This seeking and accepting forgiveness is a sacrificial process involving much "death to self", both in the forgiver and in the one forgiven.

The personal relationship between God and man is broken by Sin. The relationship eternally *is*, and nothing can alter the fact; but sin effectually destroys it, and until such sin is repented of—and forgiven —the relationship remains effectually destroyed.

To the Hebrew, sin effectually broke the Covenant and put the sinner outside it. He could no longer sit down at the Lord's table. There could be no expression of peace because there was no peace. He was at war with his God. He was in a state of condemnation—of non-existence—of death. It was necessary for the sinner to make himself forgivable by penitence and the making of satisfaction. He must atone for his sin (atonement means "at-one-ment"). His penitence must be suitably expressed, and sacrifice was the only adequate means of expression.

The Sin Offering, sometimes called the Burnt Offering, was of a perfect beast from the sinner's herd which was brought to the altar in the presence of the priest. There the sinner laid his hands upon it, identifying it with himself, a sinner. The laying on of hands "transferred" the guilt which he had incurred to the sinless beast which died in his stead. Again, the blood was collected and offered, but the whole carcase was burned. There was no feast.

This atonement, the substitution of the guiltless for the guilty, was more explicit on the Day of Atonement, a later public sacrifice involving two animals, one of which—the scapegoat—was driven into the desert, to the devil, bearing the sins of the entire nation. These two basic sacrificial forms, the Peace Offering, and the Sin Offering, underlay the whole Hebrew understanding of the Covenant. Sacrifice was due to God as his right because of what it expressed. It was the main religious action of the Hebrews, all others being subsidiary to it. It expressed, maintained—and when necessary restored—the relationship between God and the chosen people of God to which the name "Covenant" had been given.

Sacrifice was not only understood as an expression of a relationship and as a means of restoration when the relationship was ruptured by sin; it was also understood as the means whereby the relationship was instituted in the first place. The Book of Exodus gives us a record (from several sources, and much edited) of the institution of the Covenant—the solemn and specific acceptance by the Hebrews of the vocation which accompanied their insights into the nature of God.

Scholars have argued much about the sources and about the historicity of this or of that in Exodus, but my concern here is rather with the vocabulary that was made ready for our Lord's use at his Incarnation, and this included the clear understanding that a new relationship between God and man (the Covenant) was instituted by sacrifice. In fact the Covenant sacrifice was a mixture of sacrifices; there were Burnt Offerings for sin and there were Peace Offerings. All were summed up in one intention, and in the record of the Covenant ceremonies that Exodus gives us, half the blood was sprinkled upon the altar, and half was sprinkled upon the people and upon the book of the Law. This expressed, with primitive eloquence, the fact that their lives depended upon the keeping of the Law, for the Law was the basis of this new, unique relationship between God and man (*Exod 24:4–8*). It was the breaking of the Law that ruptured the personal relationship of the Old Covenant for, as St Paul points out frequently, without Law there is no specific awareness of sin.

Beside the Peace Offering, the Sin Offering and the Covenant Sacrifice, there was a fourth sacrifice which we must examine briefly, also recorded in the book of Exodus. This is the Passover Sacrifice, the later observance of which became an annual custom with the Jews, and which provided the immediate context for the Passion of our Lord. The Passover was an escape from slavery, aided, as the Hebrews believed, by divine intervention in human affairs. Indeed, as Exodus makes clear, the escape was a great deal more than an escape from slave conditions; it was an escape from the threat of extinction. The Passover Lamb was eaten entire to sustain the Children of Israel on their journey out of bondage. The blood was smeared on the doorposts as a passport from death to life.

The sacrificial ideas of the Hebrews were in marked contrast to those of the surrounding world; for sacrifice was primarily a propitiatory exercise for pagans. Their gods had to be "kept sweet" with offerings, and the ideas of power being released through blood-letting, and thus made available for the operations of magicians, was commonplace and accepted practice in the corrupted religious systems which surrounded the Hebrews. But of this there was nothing in the intention of the Old Testament rites (however much individuals may have misinterpreted and sought to corrupt them). The tone of the whole business was wholly "other" than that of the surrounding world. But the principal function of Hebraic sacrifice was to provide a vocabulary, to foreshadow that which was to come; and to provide terms of reference and suitable thought-forms by which our Lord could explain his person and his ministry to man.

# 20

# Stating the Facts

The earliest account of the Last Supper, that of St Paul, written some twenty-five years after the event, reminds the Corinthian Christians: "This is what I received from the Lord, and in turn passed on to you: that on the same night that he was betrayed, the Lord Jesus took some bread, and thanked God for it and broke it, and he said, 'This is my body, which is for you; do this as a memorial of me.' In the same way he took the cup after supper, and said, 'this cup is the new covenant in my blood.' (St Matthew amplifies this: 'Drink all of you from this,' he said, 'for this is my blood, the blood of the covenant, which is to be poured out for many for the forgiveness of sins.) (*Matt 26:28*.) Whenever you drink it, do this as a memorial of me.' Until the Lord comes, therefore, every time you eat this bread and drink this cup, you are proclaiming his death." (*1 Cor 11:23–26*.)

These words of our Lord contain within their brief length a concise but complete commentary upon the meaning of the Incarnation as understood by the Christ himself. So familiar are they to the Christian that their significance is rarely perceived in its fullness. They give the meaning of the tremendous events which are to follow within a few hours of their utterance, they herald a wholly new state of being, and they institute the means whereby this state is to be expressed. To the twentieth-century European, some little research is necessary into the vocabulary and the thought-forms that have been used before their full significance becomes clear. But to a pious Jew of the first century they must have struck home with the force of a thunderbolt. To the little band of disciples, gathered together with our Lord in the upper room, their import was manifestly far too tremendous to be taken in all at once. Full realisation came slowly, the events of that week-end left them dazed and numb; the Resurrection brought with it the beginnings of understanding, but perhaps it was not until the great illumination of Pentecost that the full meaning of the Passion became clear.

"For this is my blood . . . poured out for many for the forgiveness of sins." The language is that of the Sin Offering. Our Lord refers to himself as the victim in a sacrifice. He is the perfect victim; not merely physically perfect (the criterion of perfection in animal creation), he is to be morally perfect, without sin, in his "manhood taken into God". He willingly offers himself as the guiltless substitute—the scapegoat— the sinless victim upon whom the sins of "many" are to be laid, and who is to suffer the inbuilt consequence of sin in their stead. His death is to be the means of restoring a broken relationship between God and man. The word translated into English as "many", in its original idiom as used by our Lord, implies "everybody". The sense of our Lord's words are better understood thus: "For this is my blood . . . poured out for the totality of mankind, past, present and to come, for the forgiveness of sins."

"Now he has reconciled you, by his death and in that mortal body," wrote St Paul (*Col 1:21*), and elsewhere, he wrote, "for our sake God made the sinless one into sin, so that in him we might become the goodness of God" (*2 Cor 5:21*). The death of our Lord on the Cross is to be understood as a Sin Offering—the ultimate and final Sin Offering— eternally effective for the whole of mankind because the whole of man- kind is "summed up" in the manhood of Christ. Christ crucified is the perpetual Sin-Offering that every sinner can claim as his own reconcil- ing and atoning sacrifice. The identification of the sinner with his animal offering was always incomplete, but this was in any case only the shadow of the reality. In our Lord's sacrificial death—the reality itself—the identification of every penitent sinner with the Christ is absolute.

"This cup is the new covenant in my blood." The old covenant, the relationship existing between Israel and God, as the Old Testament proclaims it, was a relationship of creature and Creator; a personal relationship representing, as we have seen, a unique insight into the things of God, and also a unique sense of vocation which was related to that insight. By the tradition which Exodus enshrines, this unique relationship was sealed with sacrificial blood. Our Lord, using these thought-forms and this vocabulary, makes it clear beyond doubt that an entirely new relationship now obtains between God and man. This is what the whole incarnate life has been about. In Christ, manhood has been taken into God. In the words of the Athanasian Creed, our Lord Jesus Christ is "perfect God: perfect man . . . who although he be God and man, yet he is not two, but is one Christ; one, however, not by conversion of Godhead into flesh, but by taking manhood into God."

The death of the Christ is a Covenant Sacrifice; what, then, is the nature of this New Relationship? The words of the same sentence, over the cup at the Last Supper, provide the answer: "Drink all of you . . . this is my blood." It is very hard for twentieth-century, western man to realise just how shocking such a thought as this was to a Jew of our Lord's own time. The idea of man taking blood was blasphemous and contrary to the Law. It was a serious offence for a Jew to eat meat with the blood in it; only heathens did that! And they perpetrated this enormity because they neither knew nor cared that the blood—signifying the life—belongs to God alone.

> "I tell you most solemnly,
> if you do not eat the flesh of the Son of Man
> and drink his blood,
> you will not have life in you." (*Jn 6:53*)

These words of Jesus provoked uproar. "After hearing it, many of his followers said, 'This is intolerable language. How could anyone accept it?' " (*Jn 6:60.*) "After this, many of his disciples left him and stopped going with him." (*Jn 6:66.*) The shock to the pious Jewish system was tremendous; in drinking blood, the Jew was deliberately taking for himself that which belongs to God alone—he was equating himself with God. And this is exactly the point!

The new relationship between God and man is that of man taken up into God. The New Israel, the new "Chosen People"—the people of the New Covenant—are those who accept such a relationship in Christ. By faith, and baptism into that faith, they are made "members" of the Christ; cells or organs of his Mystical Body. In the New

154 THE PRIESTHOOD OF MAN

Covenant, man is to become God by virtue of his incorporation into the Christ.

The Incarnation has "taken manhood into God" fully and finally in the case of our Lord's manhood, potentially in the case of those who accept what is offered in him. The life of the New Covenant is a perpetual realisation of that potential. Just as the old relationship was expressed by the Peace Offering, in which man's acknowledgement of his creaturehood was expressed in sacrifice, and at which a meal of fellowship was shared with the Almighty; so the new relationship is to be expressed in a sacrificial meal of fellowship at which man, in whom the divine potential is being realised by grace, is to feed upon the sacrificial victim, the Christ himself, and by drinking the sacred blood, is to share in that which belongs to God alone. And all this he is able to do by right, because by his faith and his baptism into that faith, sonship is conferred upon him—as St Paul puts it—by adoption.

This, then, is the substance of our Lord's brief commentary upon his coming Passion at the Last Supper. But the Supper took place within the context of Passover, and it represents the New Passover; a Passover not merely out of human bondage, but out of the bondage of Time itself. It is a journey out of creaturehood towards Godhead. The flesh of the Lamb of God is food for the present journey:

> "I am the bread of life.
> Your fathers ate the manna in the desert
> and they are dead;
> but this is the bread that comes down from heaven,
> so that a man may eat it and not die.
> I am the living bread which has come down from heaven.
> Anyone who eats this bread will live for ever;
> and the bread that I shall give
> is my flesh, for the life of the world." (*Jn 6:48-51*)

This section of this book has been given the title, "A Consideration of Heaven," and heaven has been identified with that Eternal Life which is consequent upon a living, personal relationship with God in Christ. This Life, this relationship, which is given to man, and as much undergone by man as the earthly life and being which he undergoes by nature, completely transcends every plane or order of existence. It is the error of the good and devout occultist, or of his Eastern brother the Hindu, to regard creation as if it were like an onion. The hard outer skin of this material world is penetrated, and layer after layer is pealed away in the endeavour to reach the "god" in the middle. But God is not there—not like that. The whole onion is "in God". Heaven, the totality of which is beyond the comprehension of moral man, begins, for man, in this life because it is not to be understood as "another place to go" but as the intimate knowledge of God as he is revealed in Christ. As our Lord said:

> "I tell you most solemnly,
> everybody who believes has eternal life."
>
> (*Jn 6:47*)

# 21

# The Risen Life

"There is no known depiction of the Crucifixion until after the time of Constantine the Great and at the end of the fourth century or the opening of the fifth century." So writes C. E. Pocknee in his Alcuin Club Tract, "Cross and Crucifix in Christian Worship and Devotion".[1] He continues: "The references in St Ignatius of Antioch (c. A.D. 110) and St Justin Martyr (c. A.D. 160) to Sunday as the day of the Lord's resurrection clearly indicate the emphasis on the triumph of Christ over sin and death. Hence any depiction of Christ crucified would have been an anachronism. There was no reluctance to portray the human figure in Christian art in the second and third centuries as we can see in the Roman frescoes; but the complete absence of any depiction of the events connected with our Lord's Passion and of the Crucifixion itself cannot be accidental; and it accords with the emphasis on the resurrection and glorification of Christ."[2]

A subtle change in the focus of Christian devotion, as far as the Western Church was concerned, began to take place from the fourth century onwards. A devotion to the saving Passion, partly sentimental in character and largely subjective, developed with increasing emphasis until by the high Middle Ages, the Passion and Death of our Lord, and the penitential exercises and devotions connected with their veneration, had quite upset the balance of Christian theology in the West. This imbalance was apparent in church architecture, with great Roods focusing the devotion of the Faithful upon the Passion, while the Eucharist (heavily weighted in their understanding, as a Sin-Offering) proceeded silently and in a foreign tongue behind the screen. The

[1] C. E. Pocknee, *Cross and Crucifix*, p. 33.
[2] *Ibid.*, p. 38.

Reformed traditions continued, in the main, with a Passion-centred theology and, with the rediscovery of the Old Testament, tended to take the early Old Testament picture of the Almighty as a wrathful tribal deity uncritically. A more grotesque distortion of the simple, joyful proclamation of the Resurrection and the reality of the Risen Life which characterised the early Church, can hardly be imagined! In the early Church, let us be reminded once again; "any depiction of Christ crucified would have been regarded as a kind of anachronism!" A confusion between the "means" and the "end" has characterised the Western Church from almost the beginning.

One of the early Fathers of the Church stated, boldly, that: "God became man in order that man might become God!" Our Lord took flesh of the Blessed Virgin Mary, at his Incarnation, in order that he might ascend to heaven taking with him our humanity, with everything that this implied for creation. The Incarnation was the means, the Ascension was the end! Our Lord died upon the Cross in order that he might rise from the dead having "harrowed hell", cast out the "prince of this world", and revealed death to be at an end. The Passion was the means, the Resurrection was the end! It behoves the Baptised, both corporately as the institutional Church, and individually, to attend to the end rather than the means, and only see the means in terms of the end. The Baptised are called to live the Risen Life which has already begun in them. They must therefore seek, consciously, to identify themselves with the Risen Lord. The Resurrection, and not the Crucifixion, must be the focus of the devotion of the Baptised. It is not possible fully to lead the risen life unless this is so.

St Paul condemned "Hymenaeus and Philetus, the men who have gone right away from the truth and claim that the resurrection has already taken place". (*2 Tim 2:18*). Their error lay in supposing that, in some esoteric fashion, the Baptised are already "risen from the dead". So they are! But not like that! A relationship has been established, and the Baptised are called to lead the Risen Life which has already begun in them, but which will not attain its plenitude in this life. Its potential is to be increasingly realised by the action of Divine Grace, and it will increasingly transcend and fulfil the ordinary earthly life of the Baptised, until they can begin to acknowledge, with St Paul, that "I live now not with my own life but with the life of Christ who lives in me." (*Gal 2:20.*) Our Lord's High Priestly Prayer, on the eve of his Passion, was both an invocation of Reality and a statement of it. That potential which is to be realised by Grace is that for which our Lord explicitly prayed when he said:

> "Father, may they be one in us,
> as you are in me and I am in you,
> so that the world may believe it was you who sent me.
> I have given them the glory you gave to me,
> that they may be one as we are one.
> With me in them and you in me,
> may they be so completely one
> that the world will realise that it was you who sent me
> and that I have loved them as much as you loved me."
> (*Jn 17:21–23*)

We are concerned with man's exercise of that priesthood which is his by virtue of his place in Nature, and, in fulfilment of this, by virtue of his identification with the Eternal High Priest at his Baptism. To seek a suitable illustration, or image, to help place man in the scheme of things, and, to avoid the inbuilt danger of all images—to restrict and inhibit—I shall take a different one from any I have used hitherto. Imagine a triangle: better still, add a third dimension and visualise a pyramid.

It is normal practice, among people who build pyramids, to begin at the bottom and work up. With apologies to them, I shall begin at the top and work down, adding the courses of masonry in reverse.

The apex, the sharp point on the top of the pyramid, may be identified with a man's "ego", that which is of the essence of his own self; that inner thing which he calls "me". Below this, tiny, apex is the next course which is also relatively small, and this is to be identified with the individual's conscious mind. Between this and the courses beneath there is a kind of "damp course", an insulation of some kind which psychology calls "the threshold of consciousness". Beneath this barrier there lie an almost infinite number of courses of the masonry of which the pyramid is built, and they open out wider and wider as they proceed downwards. First, below the "damp course", likes the individual sub-conscious which is considerably larger in extent than the conscious mind above it. Then comes the group or family unconscious followed by, perhaps, the tribal unconscious, the national or racial unconscious, and so on until the whole of creation, every point of time, all history, and every "wavelength" of the world—indeed its whole within—is embraced and included in the structure, and the base of the pyramid is lost in the unformed and undifferentiated energy which is potential to the creative dynamic of Almighty God.

This image of the pyramid has, as its apex, the ego of the individual man. A man may see himself thus:

> "Myself (of which I make so great
> A fuss) is a mere, brittle spike
> Of consciousness on the circumference of being;
> A tiny terminal of an unplumbed depth."[1]

But if we would see the relationship between men, in this Natural order, in terms of our pyramidal image, then we must attempt to visualise an immeasurable number of pyramids, all sharing the same base, all in fact the same pyramid until the top two or three courses are reached. The individuals begin to differentiate at the levels, say, of the tribal and family unconscious, and are clearly separate and identifiable at the ascending levels: individual unconscious, threshold of consciousness, conscious mind and ego.

A number of realities are proclaimed by such an image as this, naïve though it is. The first is the obvious fact that all men, regardless of race, colour, age, generation or creed are brothers and share a common "foundation". All men share what psychology calls the "collective unconscious", but which is more satisfactorily described as the Universal Unconscious. At this level, all men are one, and there is communication between them at this level. Furthermore, the integrity not only of individuals, but of families and groups, tribes or clans, nations and races is proclaimed and these integrities are perceived to be objective facts demanding recognition and acceptance. But, individual though its application may be, one fact common to all men is that

[1] A. D. Duncan, *Over the Hill*, p. 25.

barrier known as the "threshold of consciousness". This is, in part at least, a product of the Fall, for the conscious awareness of, and commerce with, other dimensions and wavelengths is severely inhibited in Natural man. Some such commerce is possible, to some people, and it is the earnest endeavour of occultism, for example, to penetrate this threshold as deeply as possible. But the threshold of consciousness is a protection as well as an inhibition. It may be said to protect both ways, for its deliberate rupture, either by the use of hallucinogenic drugs, or by various practices which we may describe as "dabbling in the occult", can produce, for the individual, results which vary from the alarming to the totally disastrous. If a naïve illustration be sought, such attempts to rupture the threshold, and "let in" what lurks beyond, may be likened to by-passing the Electricity Board and attaching one's electric hair-rollers direct to the High Tension wires!

But the pyramid I have described is one pyramid only. There is another. Seek to visualise a pyramid of near-infinite dimensions supporting on its apex another pyramid, apex to apex, upside down! The lower one represents earth, the upper one is Heaven. But things are not quite as they seemed to be at first sight; the lower one is not holding up the higher, it is in fact suspended from it, and it is derivative of it.

Man, the very apex, is the point of contact between Heaven and earth. He is a priest in that he stands between the two and is the door through which all commerce passes either way. And the effect of the Fall was to cut off the traffic and close the door. Our Lord opened it again, permanently, and man in Christ, the Baptised, is a channel of Grace and it is his place so to identify his own ego with the Risen and Ascended Christ (which is, to that ego, a Crucifixion), that through him—through the Christ who lives within him—the whole of the work of reconciliation begun by our Lord may be completed.

It is the lot of all illustrations that they are misleading, and if we hold to them too faithfully, then we will be misled. Already something is wrong with our image. There is an inconsistency; for this "bottom pyramid" embraces the whole of creation—the world upon its every wavelength. The Fall affects only the wavelength from which man fell, and that to which he is now fallen. Our illustration is only apt, as it stands, for these circumstances. How best shall we illustrate to ourselves the way things truly are? And having done so, how may we relate our image of the two pyramids to this new illustration?

The "Star of David" is a six-pointed star and it is made up of two triangles, one upright and the other inverted, both contained either within the other. If a third dimension is added to this image, there are two pyramids in total union and harmony either with other. Heaven and earth are in complete and all-embracing rapport and equilibrium. But on the affected wavelengths with which I am concerned, it is as if the two pyramids are separate, with the ego of man as the only possible channel of communication and Grace. Both illustrations are thus valid. The complete union of pyramids represents "As it was in the beginning . . . and ever shall be"; and the separated pyramids represent the "is now" of our present condition, in process, as it is, of restoration into the greater wholeness.

Life abounds upon an infinite number of wavelengths; the Fall is thus a "local problem". It is, however, unique; an angelic failure into which man was caught up, inevitably, but culpably none the less. The Fall took place in Heaven in the first instance, and affected only the wavelength from which man fell, and that to which he is now fallen. The Priesthood of man thus embraces the wavelengths with which he is concerned, it does not extend to the whole creation. But in respect of those wavelengths with which man is concerned, they correspond more closely than man might suppose, and in some places this coincidence is more apparent than in others, to those with eyes to see. But man's pollution and despoilation of his own environment is limited to his own, fallen, wavelength. He has no power to despoil the world as it truly is.

F

# 22

# The Eucharist and
# the Mind of Christ

The identification of the Christ with his Church is not merely the identification of Christians with Jesus; rather, it is their identification—both as individuals and as a corporate body ("the Church")—with the title and the functions of the Christ. This is a matter of very great importance indeed. The Church is the "New Israel", the new "People of God", the company of the Faithful who, by Baptism have been objectively perfected by Grace (however imperfect they manifestly are, and on this earth remain!), and who are taken up into God by their Baptism into the Risen and Ascended Lord. This is a twofold state of affairs; it is, objectively, a state of being. But on this earth it is still a state of becoming. We might understand Baptism as representing "status" and the Eucharist as representing the activity proper to that status.

The vocation of the Church, the corporate body of the Baptised, is to be, above all else, the Eucharistic Community; the community that lives and constantly abides within the context of the Passion and Resurrection of the Christ. The "breaking of bread" (*Acts 2:46*) in the Eucharist is their only, dominically commanded, corporate act. It is the expression of what they are and of the New Relationship (or Covenant) which they represent. It is the expression, in time—in the context of this wavelength—of what the Church is. And it is the invocation of Reality and wholeness; it is in itself a union and a reconciliation of Heaven and this fallen earth.

The Church is the Eucharistic Community. It is in this sense, and this sense alone that the word "Church" is used in this book. The

Eucharist is the expression of what the Church is—indeed, it is not too much to say that it is what the Church on earth is for. It expresses the new order of existence—restored and more than restored—which she represents. But it is more than being merely the expression in the here and now of the New Covenant; it is the objective invocation and realisation in the present moment of an eternal reality. The Cross is in the very heart of God; the Lamb is "slain from the foundation of the world" (*Rev 13:8* R*V*). The death of the Christ on the Cross expressed in the fullness of time, and for all time, this eternal reality. The Eucharistic memorial made upon the altars of the Church is an expression of the same reality because, in a very real sense, it is the same expression.

It will be easier for us to grasp this important fact if we realise that the words "do this as a memorial of me" (*1 Cor 11:24–25*)—or as the Book of Common Prayer has it, "in remembrance of me" (Or *Missa Normativa*, in memory of me)—do not mean in the very least what they appear to mean at first sight! In contemporary English usage, the idea of "remembrance", "memorial", "memory", has become a subjective and backward-looking one. It evokes in the imagination such things as funeral parlours and cenotaphs and a wistful and sentimental recollection of the "good old days". Such an understanding as this of the Eucharistic memorial would be utterly grotesque. Our Lord's use of the word is objective and immediate. The Eucharist is a Sacrament: "do this" and something objectively happens; "do this" and the Father will act; the earthly action is underwritten in Heaven.

When the Eucharist is done "as a memorial of me" the eternal reality of the sacrifice of the Christ is made manifest in the here-and-now. It is often maintained that our Lord's work was done in Time and was unique and unrepeatable. The truth of this assertion is only manifest if it is clearly understood as meaning that the work of the Incarnate Life in Time was the expression of an eternal reality, and this self-same reality is expressed and objectively invoked in the Eucharistic memorials perpetuated throughout Time upon the altars of the Church.

There is a sense in which the nuptial and sacrificial characters of the Eucharist, which we have considered earlier, are subjective.

Objectively, as the very expression of the life and being of the Church, we may understand it thus: First, it is the great invocation of the Parousia, the objective bringer-in of the New Age. John, on Patmos, saw not what shall be but what *is*. The Eucharist is the wedding feast of the Lamb. Second, the Eucharist is a microcosm of the Eternal Mind in which all things abide. It is a microcosm of the Great Dance with the Cosmic Christ, the Lord of the Dance, presiding at his own mysteries. Thirdly, the Eucharist is the meeting-place of Heaven and earth and is the "earthing" of the heavenly dynamic upon earth.

The Eucharist is addressed to God the Father by God the Son in his Church. In his earthly Body in the here-and-now—the company of the Baptised, met together in the Spirit—the Christ offers himself in that selfsame, once-for-all offering as both Priest and Victim. The eternal and the here-and-now are made one; the identification of the Christ and his Church is absolute. "There you are on the altar, there you are in the chalice," said St Augustine (A.D. 354–430) to his congregation. "The whole Christ, in the Eucharist, offers the whole Christ," says Dr E. L. Mascall, and he says elsewhere, "There is one prayer, the great Eucharistic Prayer, which simultaneously consecrates and offers in one action; which offers by consecrating and consecrates by offering, and does both by giving thanks."

At the Eucharist, the veils that separate Heaven and earth are drawn away. The passage of Time gives place to the Eternal Now; becoming gives place to being; and the Baptised are at every Eucharist that ever was or ever will be, are in the Upper Room, are at the foot of the Cross, are before the throne of God where stands the Lamb "with the marks of slaughter upon him." (*Rev 5:6 NEB.*)

The Eucharist represents the whole life of the Baptised. It is the objective expression of Reality. It is the objective expression of their identification with the Christ. It is the only act of worship which they are bound to offer, and in making Eucharist they draw the whole of creation into their life and activity in Christ. The Eucharist is the primary expression of the priesthood of the Baptised, and in it the reconciling work begun at our Lord's Incarnation is complete and fulfilled. The Eucharistic Community on earth is only ever a part of the whole company of the Baptised on earth, but all the Baptised share in its offering for the whole of the life of the Baptised is Eucharist.

In his own private devotions, and especially in meditation, the Baptised continues with what we may call "the Eucharist in little". For in his prayer, in Christ and through Christ, made in the power of the Holy Spirit, he offers himself and all that with which he is associated to God the Father. This "eucharistic" activity is a fundamental part of the exercise of that priesthood of which he is partaker by being man in the first place, and above all, by being man Baptised. His meditation begins and abides within the recollection that the Baptised relationship makes possible; he is transfixed, through every level of his consciousness and being, by the light and the love of the Christ which passes through him and through everything to which he is priest, to the very heart of creation itself. He meditates in fellowship with all the blessed in Christ of every generation, age, race and creed, and also in fellowship with those others, his brethren, the Holy Angels. He is called to identify his ego, by a deliberate act of will, with the Risen and Ascended Christ and to be a channel of Grace. This is the Risen Life. This is the great reality of the Eucharist, and this is the "Eucharist in little" which must be the private devotion of the Baptised. These things already are; all he has to do is to invoke what already is.

Prayer, for the Christian, is an act of will. He does not tell the Almighty what to do! He identifies himself, by act of will, with the love of God for those for whom he prays; in so doing he becomes what he is, a channel of Grace. The prayers of the Baptised become less and less merely his own. (Indeed they are never merely his own.) As he grows in identification with his Lord, so his prayers become more and more a participation in the prayer of the corporate mind of Christ.

God created man to have, within the limits of the created order, an integrity, an autonomy, a distinct and unalterable personality which is unique in all eternity for every human being. Man is not to be altered or modified; he is to be fulfilled and perfected. Man is not to be pushed into conformity with a "master-mind"; man is not to toe the line or perish. Rather, man is to attain to perfect freedom and perfect fulfilment by becoming truly and wholly identified with the mind of Christ, while remaining fully and eternally himself.

The mind of Christ is a corporate mind in the same way that the Body of Christ is a "corpus". We are to partake of that mind, in our fulfilment, just as our partaking of that Body at Baptism is to be fulfilled. Man is baptised into both. In our earthly condition we partake of the Universal Unconscious, but in our fulfilment we shall partake of the Universal All-Conscious, which is the Mind of Christ, in which our freedom is absolute and our identification with our Lord complete.

It may be observed in the Saints, and it is the case with the Holy Angels, that their minds, though autonomous, are the Mind of Christ. In the exercise of their own complete freedom and autonomy, they act wholly in character with that Mind. Thus, their wills possessing the freedom which comes with total union with their Lord, their thoughts are Christ's thoughts, and their wills are his, and they are complete persons in their own right. Thus it is that the Saints and the Holy Angels are effective means of Grace to men.

The character of prayer is often misunderstood. It is not enough for a man to offer thanksgiving prayers; he must become thanksgiving. It is not enough for him to adore; he must become adoration. It is not enough for him to intercede; he must become intercession. I say, "it is not enough"; it is indeed enough and pleasing to God that man should offer these prayers, but the end product of that process which is the Risen Life on this earth is that he shall become prayer.

In the Eucharist, and in the truly "eucharistic" life of prayer, the Baptised lives the Risen Life, his Priesthood is exercised, and everything that he is and does becomes Eucharist; for in all these things it is the Christ who is at work in and through him.

# 23

# A Chapter of Unfamiliar Affirmations

The Fall condemned man to the conditions obtaining upon this wavelength. We have no knowledge of those obtaining upon that from which he fell, but chief among the characteristics of life on this wavelength is the constant cycle of birth and death.

To Christians, the idea of reincarnation or rebirth is an immediately alienating concept, and not without good reason. The Church has never explicitly condemned the doctrine, but she has come close to doing so on more than one occasion. The Councils of Lyons (1274) and Florence (1439) in particular rejected the doctrine by implication by affirming that, upon departure from this life, souls go either to heaven, purgatory or hell. The doctrine may have found a measure of favour with the great second-century theologian, Origen (185–254), but Origen is known better by what he is supposed to have said than what he is positively known to have said. He held a doctrine of the pre-existence of souls, but it is not always clear what, in Origen's fertile mind, was firm conviction and what was provocative speculation. His friends were many and influential; his enemies were somewhat more so.

Plato and Pythagoras held to the doctrine of reincarnation, and it is commonplace in Hinduism, Buddhism and, at times, in Qabalistic Judaism. It is a widespread belief in most primitive religious systems. The doctrine seems, at first sight, to be at variance with the Christian Revelation, and to deny both the objectivity and permanence of Baptism into a new and eternal relationship with God in Christ, and also the fundamental Christian belief in the Resurrection of the body. Reincarnation, perceived as a mechanical process, part of an impersonal world-system such as that generally held in Hinduism and Buddhism, is anathema to the Christian. A kind of "cosmic computer" which auto-matically and mindlessly spews back into incarnation a human soul, complete with a Karmic crime-sheet to work off, seems to the Christian to be an abomination and to belong less to a loving God than to the devil. An abomination such a mechanism would be indeed; but this is not the way things are. Correctly understood, not from the standpoint of the fallen human wavelength but from that of heaven, the doctrine of reincarnation can present a very different appearance and tends, far from denying the Christian Revelation and the objectivity of its Sacra-ments, rather to positively affirm them.

Reincarnation (or Rebirth) is an integral part of the nature of the created order as man knows it. It is a part of the process of evolution, and it is the means whereby souls evolve in the natural order. This is the case not only with men, but also with all living creatures at every level of evolution. It is the way of creaturely perfection in the natural order.

The evolution of man, as far as the physical vehicle only is concerned, has taken place in the manner generally accepted and understood by science. Spiritually, however, man only entered this process when a man-like creature had evolved for him to inhabit, and with which he could be identified. Man had been in existence, on another wavelength, long before this. To this we have already referred.

The evolution of man, as a spiritual being—his way of perfection in the Natural order—has been by constant rebirth since his arrival on this wavelength. Thus, in general terms, the instinctual beliefs of Hinduism, Buddhism and some other religious systems are correct. This instinctual belief was not given to the Jews of the Old Testament. Their vocation was to receive the awareness of historical process, and for this reason Our Lord had no occasion to make specific reference to this. (Such a reference would, in fact, have clouded the issues with which he dealt.) It is only now that it is necessary for Christians to come to terms with the reality of rebirth, and discover its implications in respect of the Christian Revelation.

Christ came, as he said, "not to destroy, but to fulfil". He spoke not only of the Jewish Law, but of every Law of Nature, and included in

them is the law of rebirth. For a believer, baptised into Christ, the
necessity of rebirth is done away. He is perfected, not by Nature, but
by Grace. Grace perfects and transcends Nature; there is no further
need for rebirth. Evolution is fulfilled in the Baptised.

For man, living by Nature, rebirth will continue in him and he will
ever abide within the love of God in this context. There is no question
of an unbeliever being damned eternally. Believers are called by God to
faith and Baptism; nevertheless, many are baptised who have no such
call from God. But the Church is not in error in baptising indiscrimin-
ately, for our Lord said:

> "All that the Father gives me will come to me,
> and whoever comes to me
> I shall not turn him away." (*Jn 6:37*)

The love of God knows no limitations, the Incarnation is for all men.

The Baptised have no further need for rebirth, for Baptism is objective, it confers an altogether other order of being upon man. But man
can fall from the Life of Grace, into which he has been baptised, back
to the life of Nature. This he can do by deliberate choice—his own
choice—either by unrepented Mortal Sin, or by virtue of the whole
tenor of the life he chooses to lead. He may, of his own free will,
become as if he had never been Baptised. During his current life
on earth, he may repent of either case, and be freely restored to
Grace. After his death to this life, however, the opportunity of repentance has passed and he must return to the life of Nature, to be
subsequently reborn, bearing with him the consequences of his choice
according to that principle generally known to men as Karma. In
subsequent lives, he will get other opportunities for Baptism which he
will accept or not according to the free will God gave him.

Although the Baptised have no further need to return to this wavelength, many do in fact return, voluntarily and of their own free will.
Indeed, some return many times. They do so for two reasons:

The first is in order to realise for themselves the fullness won for
them by Christ. This is the reincarnation of devotion to Almighty
God. It is a free act of love, never an act of reparation. It is impossible
for man to make reparation to God.

The second is in order to perform a specific ministry to the Glory of God and the salvation of souls. In either case, the Baptised make themselves vulnerable to all the influences of the incarnate human wavelength. They do not always reincarnate in a Christian society and they may not, consciously, be Christians during this new life. But their Baptism transcends all subsequent incarnations because they are in Christ. They may, however, fall from Grace in this new life, and, reverting to Nature, become as if they had never been baptised. Some do so revert. Not many, but some. The danger is ever present. They are greatly helped by their discarnate brethren, but their free will is inviolate, and they can choose Nature rather than Grace.

Belief in rebirth is by no means a necessary thing for a Christian. He is not concerned with it, in this life, in the very least. A Christian is called to acknowledge what de Caussade called "The Sacrament of the Present Moment". The Christian always lives now, and his concern is with the will of God for him, *now*. Nothing, in the Christian view, promises to be more uselessly Narcissistic and unproductive than the kind of speculation beloved of many devotees of the occult: "Who was I last time?" As if it mattered! What I am *now*, this very moment, is what does matter. But a theology which avoids an issue simply because it is inconvenient, or embarassing, or apparently in conflict with cherished beliefs, is simply unworthy of man's allegiance. A Christian cannot offer to God mere defensive positions with no attempts at forward reconnaisance—still less reconciliation in Christ. The evidence for the reality of rebirth is far too strong to be ignored altogether. The foregoing affirmation reveals the subject to be more straightforward than it seemed to be at first sight.

Origen, to whom I have referred, held a doctrine of the pre-existence of human souls. "He affirmed that creation was eternal in the belief that without an existing world God would have been inactive and not omnipotent. He held Him to be finite, because if He were infinite He could not think Himself. Among his most controverted theories was his teaching on souls and their destiny. All spirits were created equal, but through the exercise of their free will they developed in hierarchical order and some fell into sin and so became either demons or souls, imprisoned in bodies. Death does not finally decide the fate of the soul, which may turn into a demon or an angel. This ascent and descent goes on uninterruptedly until the final 'Apocatastasis' (salvation of all things) when all creatures, even the devil, will be saved."[1] Origen's reduction of the Almighty to the limits of human comprehension, and his confusion of the angelic order with the human, blurred his vision. Demons are rightly understood as fallen angels, but man is of an altogether different order of being. Origen's insights were profound, but wild.

The human soul is neither masculine nor feminine; it is both. Man in an androgyne. This is what our Lord meant when he said that there is neither marriage nor giving in marriage in heaven, but that men are as the angels.

Everything that exists has its own, individual soul, and its proper measure of consciousness. There is no such thing as inanimate creation; and all things are created to be eternal. It is wholly wrong, however, merely to identify Almighty God with his creation. All things are in God. It is wrong to speak of a "divine spark" in man because this gives a misleading impression of the nature of man. (It is quite proper, however, to speak of an "angelic spark" in man.) Man is a creature (like the Angels); God is the Creator.

Man has many terms by which he describes the human soul. But "Soul", "Psyche", "Higher Self", the Hindu term, Atman, and also the "Organising Field", may be identified either with other. It is as if God creates a set of proportions, unique for every creature, which the Organising Field (or Soul) expresses on every plane of being in a manner appropriate to that plane. Thus the soul is always itself and always knows itself on every plane. On the fallen human wavelength, however, man is obliged to struggle to find himself, to know himself and to become himself.

Man can only find himself in God. He can only truly become what he is by Baptism into Christ. Man cannot naturally fulfil himself; he can only be fulfilled by Grace. By Baptism, he enters into participation in the Life of Almighty God. His own life is transcended and fulfilled by the Divine Life, and he is able to become what he is; God's priest to Creation.

[1] *Oxford Dictionary of the Christian Church.*

The Fall has become a means of Grace; for man, penitent and redeemed in Christ, has been brought to an exaltation which was not his before he fell from Grace. It was to this the Christ referred when he said that there is more joy in Heaven over one sinner that repents than over ninety-nine just persons who need no repentance. The Baptised is that sinner who has repented. Man is God's priest because he shares in the eternal High Priesthood of the Christ, by his Baptism into the Christ.

Does what we have affirmed deny, either implicitly or explicitly, the fundamental Christian doctrine of the Resurrection? By no means. But we are often guilty of restricting the implications of the Resurrection to our own wavelength, and limiting it to the narrow bounds of our own concepts. We have no idea of the superabundance, or the exuberance, of Life. We would hold everything down to our own wavelength and have it stop there; we would even hold down our own wavelength and have it stop as it is because the glorious Reality is too much for us! We would call it "symbolic", very often, rather than daring to believe in it!

The Resurrection is widely misunderstood by many Christians. It is important to understand that our Lord rose, physically, from the dead on this same fallen wavelength. He had truly died upon the Cross and he truly rose from the dead. Our Lord identified this fallen wavelength with every other plane of being upon which life truly is, and began the process of its summing up and fulfilment in him, through the Priesthood of the Baptised. The Ascension of our Lord demonstrated the fulfilment of the process now begun.

We cannot, however, end our present discussion here. We must go on to ask ourselves how we are to understand Earth and its within, "Sheol", "Hades", and the dread concept of "Gehenna" which our Lord brings to our notice, and what their relationships are to Heaven? Let us state the case briefly now, and return to it as we find necessary in the chapters which follow:

Hades and Sheol—"the underworld"—are to be understood as belonging to that part of the within of creation which is proper to this fallen wavelength only. This is, as man has always known, the "abode of the dead"; their state of rest pending rebirth into this life. It is to be understood, as the Hebrews most typically understood it in the Old Testament, as an unconscious condition. However, souls could be roused to wakefulness by mediumistic and magical activity, and for this reason (and reasons connected with the practices) such activity was prohibited in Israel and made subject to extreme penalties, as the Old Testament bears witness.

Our Lord, dying on the Cross, "descended into Hell", as the Creeds proclaim—entered the abode of the dead, the underworld of this wavelength—and woke it up. "In the body he was put to death, in the spirit he was raised to life, and, in the spirit, he went to preach to the spirits in prison." (*1 Pet 3:18-19*). He led those who would accept him (including the Penitent thief) to the Paradise of Heaven which is a wholly other state of being than "earth" of any conceivable wavelength. The primitive Hebrew instinct had been wholly correct: heaven was the abode of God and his angels, and earth and its underworld was the abode of man. So they were, but no longer! Just as, at the Last Supper, man partook of that which belonged exclusively to God, so man now partakes of that wholly other state of being, in relationship with God, which we call Heaven. On this wavelength, Baptism and the Eucharist represent the "breakthrough" of Reality into the shadow.

But what of those who would not accept our Lord, and whose free will was respected, even in the underworld? They remained, conscious, in that same, continuing underworld from which rebirth into this world still continues. The deliberately, determinedly proud and rebellious still go to the underworld at death. Hell is a good name for it. They are not in torment, neither are they aware that they are not in Heaven. It is, after all, their idea of Heaven. At their next rebirth into the world, the opportunity of Baptism will again be presented. They may take it; God loves them infinitely, and their wills are free. But at our Lord's second coming, the underworld will come to an end for this wavelength will come to an end in its final reconciliation with the reality from which it fell away. Then "Gehenna"—the rubbish fire—will be a reality. The Authorised version was not so wrong, in the long run, in rendering all these underworld categories as "hell!"

The great majority of human souls go to Heaven on passing from this life. For the Baptised, the necessity for rebirth is over; for the unbaptised, the necessity still obtains. Paradise and Purgatory are subjective conditions; both of them belong to souls in Heaven.

The world-view of Hinduism and Buddhism is essentially static, as we have seen. If there is any sense of process at all, it is, as it were, a "closed-circuit" process. There is no end product in sight. But it is the whole burden of the Christian Revelation (however much neglected by Christians) that we are at the end of a very purposeful process indeed. These are the last days, as the writer of the Epistle to the Hebrews makes clear (*Heb 1:2*). The End is close at hand, when this fallen wavelength will be finally united with Reality. This is what is meant by the reference, in the New Testament, to the creation of a new Heaven and a new Earth.

# 24

# Within the Within, or Beyond?

The content of the foregoing chapter will have adequately prepared
any reader who still perseveres for surprises in this one; but the Risen
Life involves man in a great deal more than he either bargains for or is
particularly anxious to accept. Man is full of inhibitions, and the
institutional Church, being made up of men, is no less prone to them as
a kind of corporate dis-ease. Sin can be repented of, and is forgiven.
Inhibitions, which un-man us fully as seriously, are only overcome by
that grace of which St John says:

> "In love there can be no fear,
> but fear is driven out by perfect love:
> because to fear is to expect punishment,
> and anyone who is afraid is still imperfect in love."
>
> (1 Jn 4:18)

One of the manifestations of the Risen Life, of which St Paul writes,
is in the bestowal of the Gifts of the Spirit:

"There is a variety of gifts but always the same Spirit; there are all
sorts of services to be done, but always to the same Lord; working
in all sorts of different ways in different people, it is the same God who
is working in all of them. The particular way in which the Spirit is
given to each person is for a good purpose. One may have the gift of
preaching with wisdom given him by the spirit; another may have the
gift of preaching instruction given him by the same Spirit; and another
the gift of faith given by the same Spirit; another the gift of healing,
through this one Spirit; one, the power of miracles; another, prophesy,
another the gift of recognising spirits; another the gift of tongues and
another the ability to interpret them. All these are the work of one and

the same Spirit, who distributes different gifts to different people, just as he chooses." (*1 Cor 12:4–11*.)

It is astonishing how this passage can be read over and over again, through the years, without its full import being recognised. In modern terms, among the gifts listed may be recognised mediumship of many kinds, charismatic healing and various other "psychic phenomena", none of which are looked upon with favour by ecclesiastical orthodoxy in the Western Church today.

These gifts are objective and real, but they are not limited to the Baptised. Some of them work at different levels and it may well be that St Paul had in mind the perfection, by Grace, of that which is fairly commonplace in nature. Be that as it may, we are to understand that the exercise of the perceptive gifts is at its most typical among the Baptised, prayerfully and as an expression of a clear vocation in Christ. There are dangers inherent in the exercise of any gift, and these become extreme if integrity is lost by the misuse of the gift. Furthermore, the seeking after gifts of this kind which are not given by God is mere "dabbling in the occult" and attracts the retribution it deserves, but it must be understood that God gives gifts and the vocations to use them to his glory, and deliberate disuse can be as culpable as misuse.

The Western Church has always inclined towards an over-paternalistic, over-institutionalised and over-legalistic endeavour to protect people from themselves and to inhibit the exercise of anything which might involve danger to faith and order and damage to souls. This is temperamental, but it is also unfaithful. Officially, the exercise of the perceptive gifts has been recognised only in tightly controlled situations. Within this climate, both St John of the Cross and St Teresa, highly endowed though they were, preferred to "play down" the perceptive gifts. They were concerned in their writings with the states of Grace and prayer to which they sought to inspire their readers, and their reticence is natural in the circumstances in which they wrote. To see the perceptive gifts as ends in themselves, or as indicative of any particular state of grace (or of initiation into "mysteries") is grotesque. This is psychism at its worst and is open to every kind of delusion, but the perceptive gifts, recognised as Gifts of the Spirit, and used prayerfully to the glory of God in obedience to a clear vocation, are as much a manifestation of the Risen Life as those other gifts enumerated with them: preaching with wisdom, and instructing in the faith.

In an earlier chapter I mentioned the claim of many occultists that they were accustomed to becoming "contacted upon the inner planes". Some material, claimed by its authors to have been directly received through such contacting, has found its way into these pages. St Paul makes clear enough references to mediumship, as we have seen, and includes this under the heading "Gifts of the Spirit", and there is no doubt whatsoever that it is God, the Holy Spirit, who is meant in this context. It is very clear, therefore, that we are bound to seek the grace of "recognising spirits" (*1 Cor 12:10*) in order to distinguish between the various sources contacted from other planes of being. If such activities as these are realities and not mere subjective delusions, nothing is more important than this. There will be many good and devout persons who will decide, *a priori*, that this is all nonsense.

The fact is that communication from other planes of being—from souls, that is, who are no longer in this life—is a reality, and a reality beyond reasonable doubt to those who have studied the evidence. At best, it is a part of the Risen Life which can be described as "the practice of the Communion of Saints". It is, for persons in this life, something that is most typically given rather than sought. But this description of the practice at its best is to be applied with considerable caution, for at less than its best it may justly be described in terms very different indeed. Integrity, right intention, the responsible and prayerful use of the gift and the context in which it is used are of overriding importance. It is, after all, fully as desirable with this as it is desirable when using a radio set to know where the programme is coming from!

I am here obliged to return, briefly, to metaphysics. The "under-world" is the within of this fallen wavelength only. From it, the souls to whom our Lord preached during his period of earthly death were led (those who would come) to a wholly other state of being which we call Heaven, and the basis of which, as far as we are concerned, is a relationship with the Lord.

This relationship may be perceived as existing upon two levels. First is the natural level, enjoyed by every man by virtue of our Lord's incarnation. Second is the level of grace, enjoyed by the baptised, by virtue of their baptism. From Heaven, there is the possibility of communication with souls in this life through mediumship of various kinds, but it is very necessary to understand that, just as earthly life is a process, so is the Life of Heaven. The limitations of human understanding continue to apply, although the process of perfection in Grace gradually removes them.

Thus it is that any communication, mediumistically received, must be subjected to exactly the same criticism and criteria as any other human communication in this life. Sincere mistakes abound! However consciously an exercise of a gift of the Holy Spirit this might be, and however devoutly offered in prayer, people are people! And people who know little don't know much! The one dolorous aspect of the this-worldly human situation which is lacking in communicators from Paradise is intentional deceit. Mistakes, when they are made, are utterly sincere, and usually, inconsequential. The character and tone of communications is what reveals their origins most surely. Those from the Paradise of Heaven betray the essential character of that happy state; we may summarise it in three words: Life, Love and Laughter!

But I have not presented the whole picture by any means. Mediumistic activity can operate in more than one direction, for the medium is very like a radio set with more "stations" on the dial than most. And, sad to relate, occult "contact upon the inner planes", however sincerely and honestly sought, is not typically—nor perhaps very often—contact with Heaven. The very mechanisms used inhibit this! But such is the gravity of the theological error underlying occultism, that this fact is not always apparent to those within that discipline.

A normal occult technique, other than the employment of mediums, is the construction of what is known as a "telesmatic image". This is a form, constructed in the imagination either by meditational or ritual means, for a "force" to inhabit and work through. Frequently this involves the use of clairvoyant gifts which this kind of exercise naturally stimulates. The construction of a telesmatic image provides a mechanism—akin to mediumship—which can enable a person not in this life to communicate with the occultist. The unhappy facts of the case are, however, that the mechanism is very aptly constructed to contact, not Heaven, but rather the underworld! This is the within of this fallen wavelength, inhabited by the invincibly proud and power-seeking. The "contacts" therefore tend to be with those who seek "disciples" and domination; who impart "arcane knowledge" and, in the process, obtain the devotion of, and considerable control over their this-worldly disciples. It is a readily observable phenomenon that occultism in general—that is to say, as an "ism"—tends to divide and fragment. There are very many gifted and dedicated persons who practice it with great devotion and with impressive sincerity. There is much, in occult science, which is of considerable worth and many important truths are enshrined therein. It is no accident that most major branches of science owe their origins to the researches of occultists in the first instance, who researched into the earth, the world, creation, mistakenly identifying them with Heaven. But the direction in which occultism—as an "ism"—is naturally focused is quite mistaken, due to its underlying false theology.

It would be arbitrary, and it would be grotesque, to suppose that the truth never penetrates the faulty techniques of the occultist. Human sincerity and integrity can "redeem" (in the natural order) the most surprising things, and a very great deal of occult tradition is both true and manifestly so. The Qabalah, the philosophical framework within which a great many occultists work, is an inspired "map" of the general structure of the Within of creation—and I fancy more so in its Gentile, occult form than in its far more devotional Jewish original. But magic, the art of making changes in consciousness in accordance with the will, is a "lower pyramid" exercise only. Its fulfilment is in Christ—but then it is no longer magic! The manipulation of creation is a doubtful business and, at best, it is probably a wrong thing done for right reasons. The guardian angel of a sincere white magician is hard put to it to keep his charge from corruption; but to say this does not preclude all possibility of success!

. . . . .

The Christian is sometimes hard put to it to match the sheer awareness of creation and its wonders that the occultist is heir to. This,
when it is so, is tragic, for the Christian is doubly priest to creation;
by his manhood, and by his Baptism. But it has been the temptation
of Western Christendom to over-intellectualise, to go through the
motions of world-rejection and to become remote from the mud
of the good earth. The growing conurbations have made this worse
still.

All mediumistic work is fraught with the danger of some interpolation from the underworld. By the same token, we must be glad that
Heaven breaks through into the underworld communications of the
sincere occultists, saving them from some of the worst of their errors.
But even with the greatest recollection, and after the most prayerful
preparation, the possibility of interpolation and distortion is not removed altogether. Thus it is that any matter whatever which is mediumistically communicated must be subjected to the normal scrutinies of
reason, and tested against the Truth as revealed in Christ. There are
no other criteria whatsoever.

Distortions are both a problem and a source of danger, and they
can arise in three ways. In the first case, there can be "interference"
from the medium himself. This is not usually either serious or severe,
given integrity and recollection. The second source of distortion is
sheer error on the part of the communicator, but this is not usually
a serious matter, given a normally critical reception. Thirdly, there is
the more serious danger of the communication being broken into from
the underworld. A comparable illustration is the deliberate interference
and interpolation of news broadcasts during the second world war!
This was a brief and naïve effort, productive more of merriment than
of dismay. But the mechanism is comparable.

Mediumistic activity, done otherwise than in Prayer and as a
deliberate exercise of a gift of the Spirit, is wide open to every kind of
delusion and deceit, and can all too frequently merely give embodi-
ment to either the subjective subconscious desires of those present, or to
some other aspect of their group unconscious. Thus it was that, in
the beginning of this chapter, I claimed that the perceptive gifts, al-

though not confined to the Baptised, ought most typically to be used among them, in prayer, in obedience to a clear sense of vocation, and within the context of a Christian discipleship.

Departure from this life begins, as it would appear, with a kind of "intermediate state" which is earthbound and time-conscious, although not in a way relatable to our own. It is, in fact, an underworld condition, even for those destined for heaven. Not infrequently the dead fail to realise that they are dead. This intermediate state is one in which demonic torment is possible, to those who have, by their way of life, laid themselves thus open. The duration of this state may be long or short, but it is not possible to relate "duration" to earth-time. There are many people whose make-up is such that they can enter this state, at least partly, during this earthly life. This gift is much sought by esotericists—and most unwisely—under the title given to it of "Etheric travel". It is a gift natural to this wavelength, but an exceedingly dangerous one. Most of those naturally endowed with this gift are instinctively inhibited from its exercise by an awareness of its dangers.

Souls in the intermediate state are most objectively aided through it by the Eucharist, which is the invocation of Reality and of their identification with that reconciliation of Heaven and the fallen earth effected by the Christ. They are aided too by the meditations of the Baptised—"the Eucharist in little"—and by exorcism on the rare occasions when it is appropriate. They are also aided by Christian mediumistic activity in consort with souls in the Paradise of Heaven charged with this task.

I have spoken of demonic torment, but there is no need to dwell upon this. As Holy Scripture proclaims, the devil is earthbound and is confined to this fallen wavelength and that from which man fell, and also to the related underworld. Occult demonology, as recorded on an earlier page, is as merely fanciful as most things written about the devil and his angels outside the pages of Holy Scripture. If the Baptised would dwell upon these dolours, it is better for them to pray for the redemption of the devil and his angels, and leave it at that!

# 25

# In Conclusion

There must come an end to everything. The book of Job ought, perhaps, to serve as a kind of archetypal image of all theological works. After forty-one long, long chapters of human cleverness, "religion" and "moral theology", Job suddenly arrived at the moment of truth; he addressed the Almighty thus:

> "I know that you are all-powerful:
>     what you conceive, you can perform.
> I am the man who obscured your designs
>     with my empty-headed words.
> I have been holding forth on matters I cannot understand,
>     on marvels beyond me and my knowledge. . . .
> I knew you then only by hearsay;
>     but now, having seen you with my own eyes,
> I retract all I have said,
>     and in dust and ashes I repent." (*Job 42:1–6*)

At this point we have arrived in this book because it is, in a sense, about God. And nobody can write a book about God. There must come a time when argument and intellect give place to a naked and unadorned desire for God—not as we can conceive of him, but as he is in himself. Thus, in that supreme classic of Hindu spirituality, the *Bhagavad Gita*, King Arjuna addresses the Lord Krishna (who is a "type" of the Christ) thus:

> "In this mercy thou hast told me the secret supreme of thy Spirit
> and thy words have dispelled my delusion.
> I have heard in full from thee of the coming and going of beings,
> and also of thy infinite greatness.

I have heard thy words of truth, but my soul is yearning to see:
to see thy form as God of this all." *(B.G. 11:1-3)*

To his prayer, Arjuna had this answer:

"See now the whole universe with all things that move and move
not, and whatever thy soul may yearn to see. See it all as One in me.
But thou never canst see me with these thy mortal eyes: I will give
thee divine sight. Behold my wonder and glory." *(B.G. 11:7-8)*

And Sanjaya, the storyteller, tells us what Arjuna saw:

"And Arjuna saw in that form countless visions of wonder: eyes
from innumerable faces, numerous celestial ornaments, numberless
heavenly weapons;
Celestial garlands and vestures, forms anointed with heavenly
perfumes. The Infinite Divinity was facing all sides, all marvels
in him containing.
If the light of a thousand suns suddenly rose in the sky, that
splendour might be compared to the radiance of the Supreme
Spirit.
And Arjuna saw in that radiance the whole universe in its variety,
standing in a vast unity in the body of the God of gods."

*(B.G. 11:10-13)*

On an earlier page, we recognised morals and metaphysics as pro-
ceeding from mystical experience. When man is given "divine" sight
for a moment, and sees things as they truly are, he is never the same
again. And in such an experience both definitions of Mysticism come
together. The experience is Prayer, of a sort that is "given", and is a
communion with the Ultimate, however brief. Thus Buddha under
the Bo tree, and Plotinus, and Jacob at Bethel, and the unknown
author of the *Gita* all saw what it was given them to see, as did, in the
fuller dispensation, John on the island of Patmos and Paul on the
Damascus road. They are not alone. God is free with his favours, but
who can speak of them?

But the gift, for a moment, of "divine sight" is also productive of,
and part of, that Mystical Consciousness which is compelled to face
up to the facts of the world at a deeper level, and to remain conscious
of (and disturbed by) the within of things.

In these pages I have done no more than scratch a few surfaces, having once seen something, perhaps, of "the whole universe in its variety, standing in a vast unity in the body of the God of Gods." But as soon as intellect gets to work upon vision, there is a multiplication of sorrows. Lau-Tse recognised this in speaking of the Tao (the underlying principle at the heart of all things—in the language of St John, the Word):

> "Then men grew wise, invented names;
> With names for this and names for that,
> Oh! Who can find repose?
> The man who knows where lies repose
> Is free from all uncertainty.
> The Word, in this uncertain world,
> Is like a thousand little streams
> That meet, and vanish in the sea."
>
> (*Tao Teh Ching 32*)

But sorrow is of the essence of this fallen world, and Holy Scripture proclaims the tragedy of the Fall to be in the final stages of repair. But it is not mere restoration, it is recreation to a glory that did not exist before. Man, God's priest, through his Fall and re-creation in Christ, is now a creature of Heaven and High Priest, in Christ, to that which once he betrayed. Through him, a new and more glorious relationship is coming into being between God and his creation than ever was before. A new and more glorious measure is introduced into the Great Dance. It is already in being; its plenitude is not long to be delayed.

At a deeper level than even St Paul realised, there exists a kind of "cosmic dilemma"—albeit a subjective one: "Does it follow that we should remain in sin so as to let grace have greater scope?" (*Rom 6:1*) It is a measure of the infinity of God's love that this dilemma should find expression upon any level!

But the end is in view. The fallen wavelength and that from which man fell will be united and made one—and a new one; and the final reconciliation of all things will be effected. It behoves the Baptised to pray for the speedy return of the Christ in glory (if they love him, don't they want him to come?) and that Satan and his angels may be redeemed, and that all proud souls may be saved from the final extinction of the underworld, and that the worst consequences of the Fall in the Natural order may be averted by Grace.

The Christ, for whose return we pray, is, with the Father, both Transcendent and Immanent; in whom all things are, and, in particular, in the Faithful, in the Blessed Sacrament and in all things in a manner appropriate to their nature, and in the Risen and Ascended Jesus who still confronts his Faithful in an utterly personal manner as he confronted John on Patmos, and Paul on the Damascus road.

It is the loving Will of God that all things should be reconciled through the saving victory of the Crucified, Risen and Ascended Lord, and through his continuing priesthood among his Baptised in his Church.

"The one who guarantees these revelations repeats his promise:
I shall indeed be with you soon.
Amen; come, Lord Jesus."                               (*Rev 22:20*)

# Index